CW00969185

With the benefit of over 50 years of pe
rience in Japan, Boyé Lafayette De
aspects of Japanese culture which ha.. .. g.... ....
competitive edge and are worth emulating. He also alerts the reader
to opportunities, pitfalls, and "code words" to help maximize mutually beneficial relations with Japanese business partners.

— *Joe Schmelzeis, President, JPS International, Tokyo, Japan*

In his usual deft way, Japan specialist Boyé Lafayette De Mente has
not only taken the mystery out of the samurai code of ethics. He has
captured the *blue* (far, deep, sacred/sexy) and the *green* (near, shal-
low, mundane) of the Shinto-based ethos of the samurai and shown
how its positive facets can be used to dramatically enhance one's
character and skill in any undertaking.

— *Michihiro Matsumoto, author, management consultant and
President of the International Debate Development Association*

Boyé Lafayette De Mente again provides serious students of Japan
with illuminating insights into what makes the nation tick. The
opening of the Japanese market to direct foreign investment makes
this book exceptionally timely. Much has changed since Japan
opened to the outside world in the late 19th century, but the legacy
of the samurai code still conditions how Japanese business is con-
ducted. This book should become *must reading* for executives,
managers and investors doing business with and in Japan.

— *Donald Westmore, Executive Director
American Chamber of Commerce in Japan*

Other Books by Boyé Lafayette De Mente
(Partial Listing)

THE
JAPANESE
SAMURAI
CODE
Classic Strategies for Success

Positive Factors in the Samurai Code
That Enhance Skills & Performance

Boyé Lafayette De Mente

TUTTLE PUBLISHING
Tokyo • Rutland, Vermont • Singapore

Published by Tuttle Publishing, an imprint of Periplus Editions (HK) Ltd,
with editorial offices at 364 Innovation Drive, North Clarendon, Vermont 05759 and
130 Joo Seng Road, #06-01/03, Singapore 368357.

Copyright © 2004 Boyé Lafayette De Mente

All rights reserved. No part of this publication may be reproduced or utilized in any form
or by any means, electronic, mechanical, including photocopying, recording or by any
information storage retrieval system, without prior permission of the publisher.

ISBN 0-8048-3652-3
Printed in Singapore

Distributed by:

North America, Latin America & Europe
Tuttle Publishing
364 Innovation Drive
North Clarendon, VT 05759-9436
Tel: (802) 773 8930
Fax: (802) 773 6993
Email: info@tuttlepublishing.com
www.tuttlepublishing.com

Japan
Tuttle Publishing
Yaekari Building, 3rd Floor
5-4-12 Osaki, Shinagawa-ku
Tokyo 141-0032
Tel: (03) 5437 0171
Fax: (03) 5437 0755
Email: tuttle-sales@gol.com

Asia Pacific
Berkeley Books Pte. Ltd.
130 Joo Seng Road,
#06-01/03, Singapore 368357
Tel: (65) 6280 1330
Fax: (65) 6280 6290
Email: inquiries@periplus.com.sg
www.periplus.com

09 08 07 06 05
6 5 4 3 2

TUTTLE PUBLISHING® is a registered trademark of Tuttle Publishing.

Contents

Yorimasa Minamoto
(1104–1180)

Noted Aristocrat Samurai Warrior & Poet
Member of the famous Genji family, killed in battle.

Miyako ni wa
Mada aoba nite
Mishikadomo
Momiji chirishiku
Shirakawa no Seki

In Kyoto the maple leaves
were still green.
When I reached
the Shirakawa Barrier
they covered the ground.
[In a crimson carpet]

Saigyo
(1118–1190)

Noted Wandering Warrior/Monk/Poet

Oshinabete
hana no sakari ni
narini keri.
Yama no ha goto ni
kakaru shira kumo

The cherry blossoms
are flowering at their best.
The peaks and slopes
of the mountain are covered
as if by a white cloud.

Acknowledgments

I am indebted to the following for their contributions to this book:

Tokuo (Paul) Maruoka Banking Executive and Management Consultant, with over forty P/A years experiencing acting as a bridge between Japanese and Westerners.

Earle Okumura Bilingual, bicultural Management Consultant, President of Hakkoen, Inc., and an old friend whose samurai ancestors go back some thirteen generations.

Glenn Davis Tokyo-based Journalist, Author, Lecturer, and Editor who was the first to make use of computers in the publishing industry in Japan.

Sam Jameson Tokyo-based Foreign Correspondent; former *Los Angeles Times* and *Chicago Tribune* Japan Bureau Chief; Author; Lecturer.

Mutsuo Shukuya Educator, *Tanka* Poet, Author, Columnist—often described as "The fastest poet in the East" for his samurai-like ability to compose a poem in minutes.

Donald Westmore Executive Director of the American Chamber of Commerce in Japan, old Japan-hand and wise student of the ways of the Japanese.

Eric Oey Publisher, Periplus Editions, whose prodding put me on the right path.

Masumi Muramatsu Author, Lecturer, Simultaneous Interpreter for Prime Ministers, Presidents, Kings and other notables, and Japan's leading advocate of the importance of humor in business.

Dr. Michihiro Matsumoto Ex-CEO, former NHK talk show host, prolific Author (over 100 books, including the seminal *Haragei: The Unspoken Way*), Management Consultant, President of the Kodokan Debate Society, President of the International Debate Development Association, and often described as "the most dangerous man in Japan" because he always asks "Why?"

Joe Schmelzeis, Jr. President, JPS International, Inc., Corporate Management Consultant, Tokyo. I am especially indebted to Joe Schmelzeis, who was raised in Japan, and whose bilingual and bicultural qualifications, combined with his business experience in Japan and studies of Bushido [the theme of his MBA thesis at Harvard Business School], made his critique of the manuscript especially valuable.

Preface

BUSHIDO (Buu-she-doh), the ethical system of Japan's famous samurai class, which ruled the country from 1192 until 1868, eventually came to encompass every aspect of the lives of the people—their philosophical and spiritual beliefs, their etiquette, their family life, their dress, their work, their aesthetic sense, even their recreation.

Over generations, the culture of the samurai became so deeply embedded in the consciousness of the Japanese that it was difficult, if not impossible, for them to think outside of its parameters. The control it exercised over their attitudes and behavior was virtually infinite.

But there was a fatal weakness in the samurai culture as an economic, political and social system. It was able to survive in its full form only in the closed, exclusive environment that existed in Japan during those long centuries.

The opening of Japan to the Western world, beginning in 1854 when the first trade and diplomatic agreement was signed with the United States, was the death knell for the Shogunate—the samurai system of government.

By 1868, the Shogun had been overthrown and by 1876, the samurai class had been abolished, leaving the Japanese without the cultural and structural anchor that had given them balance and purpose for nearly a millennium.

The samurai government of Japan failed to survive the opening of the country to the outside world because its primary tenets were incompatible with a profit-making economy, with individualism and personal initiative, and with change—not to mention its basic inhumanity.

And yet, the influence of the Bushido code of ethics played the key role in the making of modern Japan between 1870 and 1895. It was samurai from provinces that were more distant from the Shogunate capital in Yedo (Tokyo) who brought the downfall of the warrior class; it was samurai who restored the Emperor to the Throne; it was samurai who brought the Industrial Revolution to Japan and managed it from the top.

The goal of the new post-Shogunate government of Japan, dominated by ex-samurai, was to retain the spirit of the samurai and to catch up with and bypass the West economically and militarily. The rest, as the saying goes, is history.

It was, in fact, the samurai culture that made it possible for Japan to achieve extraordinary economic and military success from 1870 to the debacle of the war with the United States in the 1940s, and to rebound from that defeat and destruction in less than thirty years and, astoundingly, become the second largest economy in the world.

The ex-samurai leaders of the new Japan, most from the lower ranks of the samurai class, simply adapted the clan system and the samurai code of behavior to the creation of modern-appearing industrial combines and to a new national military force attired in Western style uniforms instead of kimono and armed with Western weapons instead of swords (although officers in the new military forces carried both).

The influence of the samurai code of ethics on Japan's arts, crafts, literature, poetry and other aesthetic and intellectual pursuits remained virtually intact over the next several decades, continuing to imbue them with a distinctive character that is found only in Japan. The code also gave the Japanese traits that made it possible for them to create an economic superpower based on manufacturing products that within one decade were as good as or superior to those being made in other countries, and exporting them in huge volume to the markets of the world.

By 1990, however, the samurai code of ethics that had shaped and controlled the lives of the people for so many generations had been obscured by a Western façade and appeared to have lost much of its vitality. Unwise monetary policies and fundamental shifts in economic conditions in Japan and internationally conspired to take some of the steam out of the country's mighty Bushido-code-driven manufacturing and exporting industries.

The implosion of Japan's bubble economy in the early 1990s was a shock of enormous proportions to the Japanese who had been convinced for the previous thirty years that their indomitable Bushido spirit was going to carry them to greater heights of economic success.

On the business and political front, the unbounded confidence the Japanese had exhibited during their rise to economic superpower status spiraled downward. But the code they had lived by for centuries was not gone. A knowing eye could still see it in the daily behavior of the people everywhere—in the shops, department stores, factories, hotels and offices.

Over the next decade the feeling that the spirit of the samurai should be officially revived began to grow. Many began to preach that doing so was imperative if Japan was to continue to survive and prosper in the 21st century.

Bushido: The Soul of Japan, written by Inazo Nitobe over a hundred years ago, and published in 1905, was suddenly in such demand that several new editions were published—some in Japanese and some in English. While very insightful and informative, Nitobe's book is almost an apology for the samurai code, as his approach was to compare virtually every attribute of the way of the samurai with that of the knights of England and other European countries during the Middle Ages—with emphasis on the equivalent warts of the latter.

In fact, Nitobe has long been a national hero in Japan, not for his efforts to explain Bushido to the Western world, but for all of the other writings he did in a valiant attempt to bridge the cultural gap between Japan and the West. As Japan-hand Joe Schmelzeis notes: "Nitobe's face has long graced the ¥5,000 note—even though most Japanese have no idea why he is there."

By the year 2000, the unofficial revival of the samurai spirit had begun in earnest, and was taking a number of forms. One of these forms was a movement, especially among the young and among women in particular, to return to the philosophical and spiritual code of the samurai culture by taking up training with the sword, long the primary symbol of the warrior class.

Another classic work on Bushido, *HAGAKURE: The Book of the Samurai*, dictated by retired samurai Tsunetomo Yamamoto between 1710 and 1716, was republished in English in 2002, and quickly became a bestseller. [*Hagakure* translates as "In the Shadow of Leaves," a typical Japanese way of using poetic and esoteric expressions when referring to things.]

Hagakure is not a treatise on the samurai code of ethics; rather, it is a collection of sayings by samurai, and descriptions of incidents relating to samurai behavior. [Among other things, it is an omen of some of the ugliest and most pathological forms of behavior that later Japanese were to demonstrate in their domestic and foreign wars.]

All one has to do today to witness the survival and persistence of many of the positive and beneficial patterns of behavior epitomized in the Bushido code is visit any Japanese department store, any inn or traditional restaurant, any factory, or any government office, as well as any of the large and famous international hotel chains, and there you will see the legacy of Bushido in action.

And yet, only a tiny percentage of the younger generation is making an effort to return to the positive elements of the Bushido code. The traditional characteristics of the Japanese are therefore growing weaker year-by-year, and that is having an increasingly negative impact on the samurai-based traits that made them such a formidable people.

In this book, I have attempted to identify the positive factors in Bushido that were primarily responsible for the astounding economic success of the Japanese, and still today play a vital role in their economic prowess. I believe that Japan must take dramatic steps to reintroduce the positive elements of the Samurai Way to the younger generations if Japan is to maintain its preeminent place in the world community.

Many of these samurai-inspired cultural factors also provide valuable lessons for people around the world, not only in business but in all other pursuits as well, including striving for a graceful life. The positive elements in the Bushido code are, in fact, a manual for success.

Boyé Lafayette De Mente

1

The Power of the Samurai Culture

Kyoui no Bushi Bunka
(K'yoh-we no Buu-she Boon-kah)

No Westerner has ever spent more than a few days in Japan without becoming aware of something that is subtle and seemingly mysterious about Japanese culture—something that makes itself felt despite the cacophony of sounds, neon signs and other garish sights that make up the more conspicuous modern-day façade of the country.

This subtle "something" that most visitors see and feel when they are exposed to Japanese culture derives from a variety of traditional arts, crafts and customs that have survived into modern times and now exist alongside the artifacts and styles imported from the West.

What visitors to Japan are seeing and feeling is the essence of what makes these things Japanese, an essence that is made up of a combination of extraordinarily refined physical beauty, the spirituality inherent in the various materials concerned, along with the attitude and behavior of the people.

These special attributes of Japanese culture, all traceable in varying degrees to the influence of the samurai code of ethics, have a hypnotic-like appeal for most Westerners, especially long-term or permanent residents, including a significant number who are simultaneously repelled by other aspects of "The Japanese Way" that offend their own cultural biases and personal prejudices.

A long time ago the Japanese recognized that the physical and spiritual worlds are essential to each other, and separating or unbalancing them results in disharmony, which can easily and quickly become destructive. This ancient wisdom was incorporated into all aspects of the daily lives of the Japanese, ranging from religious rituals and festivals to all of the mundane acts of existence, including the preparation of food, eating, and the learning and practicing of arts and crafts.

Skill Plus Spirituality

As was also characteristic of traditional Japanese culture, this aspect of Japanese life was precisely defined and labeled, so it could be discussed, understood, taught and passed on from one generation to the next. These particular labels were *do* (doh) and *waza* (wah-zah). *Waza* by itself means "skill", while *do*, usually translated into English as "way", means much more than what the English word suggests. It incorporates both the physical and metaphysical—with the spiritual factor often being more important than the physical.

In other words, the Japanese approach to life combined developing physical skill as well as spirituality. There was no area of Japanese life that did not have its own *waza* and *do*. Whether taught by parent, teacher, or craft master, every skill was instilled with its own special spiritual component that frequently transcended the physical realm. So important was the spiritual side of training and learning in Japan that it overshadowed the physical side, eventually becoming ritualized in such terms and endeavors as *Bushi Do* (Way of the Warrior), *Cha Do* (The Way of Tea), *Karate Do* (Way of the Empty Hand), *Kendo* (the Way of the Sword), and so on.

In addition to the *do* of martial arts, fine arts and a variety of institutionalized aesthetic pursuits, the learning and practicing of virtually every other activity in Japan was based on following minutely prescribed forms and processes known as *kata* (kah-tah), which translates as "form", "process" or "way of doing things".*

Under the influence of the powerful samurai culture, Japanese behavior was structured into carefully patterned movements that were highly stylized and related to the class, sex and age of the individual in a vertically ranked society in which conformity to "appropriate" behavior often took precedence over the purpose of the action.

Because there was a recognized and ritualized way of doing virtually everything in Japanese society, and the teaching and following of these ways were performed with religious devotion, the standards of behavior in general and in all work skills became very high.

The skills and discipline instilled into individual Japanese by their *waza/do* culture were key elements in their extraordinary art, craft and aesthetic accomplishments, as well as in their rise to economic prominence in modern times.

The values that gave birth to and sustained Japan's spiritually imbued culture have changed dramatically since the end of the feu-

---

* For a definitive look on the origin and influence of the *kata* factor in Japanese life, see the author's *KATA—The Key to Understanding and Dealing With the Japanese* (Tuttle Publishing Company).

dal system in 1945/6. However, so powerful was this ritualized, orchestrated way of life that still today enough of it remains to distinguish the Japanese and provide them with a number of comparative advantages in competing with other people.

A story told by ex-samurai Tsunetomo Yamamoto (1659–1719) after his fief Lord Katsushige died illustrates the incredible hold that Bushido had on the minds and behavior of the samurai class. When Yamamoto was ordered not to commit *harakiri* to follow his lord in death, he gave up the calling of samurai, became a monk and began dictating his memoirs. He recalled that when Lord Katsushige was fifteen years old his father ordered him to go to the fief's execution ground near the western gate of his castle and "cut" several prisoners who had been condemned to death to get practice in beheading men. "Cut" was the word used to mean "kill" because cutting with a sword was the usual way of killing. Ten convicted felons were lined up in a row. The fifteen-year-old boy cut the heads off nine of them in rapid succession. When he came to the tenth man, who was described as young and healthy, the young samurai stopped and said: "I'm tired of cutting now. I will spare this man's life."

Reviving the Samurai Culture

One of the most compelling challenges facing Japan today is how to prevent the further weakening of the positive aspects of the samurai culture. The last remaining bastions teaching the "Japanese Way" are the various schools teaching the aesthetic pursuits and martial arts for which the Japanese are famous, and companies whose managers continue to see value in the traditional ways.

The result of this ongoing behavioral training in Japanese companies as well as in private and professional schools is especially visible in the hospitality industries, where Japan's traditions of service have historically been honed to the highest level.

While most Japanese businessmen recognize the value of the samurai approach to life, only a few of the larger firms have well-defined in-house training programs designed to instill the best of these traditional virtues into their employees.

Still, it is fairly common to visit well-known, internationally oriented Japanese firms and be treated with the same stylized manners and hospitality that marked the long centuries of the country's feudal period under the samurai government.

At a recent luncheon in a Japanese style restaurant in an ordinary Tokyo hotel, I was made acutely aware of how such behavior distinguishes the Japanese way of doing ordinary things, and the extraordinary feelings of confidence, appreciation and admiration this kind and quality of behavior engenders in those who are sensitive to such things.

I was also strongly reminded that what I was seeing and experiencing was the reason why the Japanese are such formidable people; and that their success, to a substantial degree, is the result of the samurai-based intensive training, extraordinary diligence, and an emotional-spiritual commitment that sets them apart from most other people.

The subtle, mysterious-appearing qualities of Japanese culture that impress and sometimes confuse Western visitors are, in fact, nothing more than the visible manifestations of an artistically and spiritually defined culture that in many respects was taken to the extreme—and which is sometimes beyond the understanding of modern-day Japanese as well.

However, the positive aspects of Japanese culture, which are no more than a combination of common sense, folk wisdom, intellectual sophistication, aesthetic appreciation and diligence, are certainly worthy examples that the rest of the world would do well to emulate.

Says Tokuo (Paul) Maruoka, banker and business consultant: "The teachings and spirit of Bushido do in fact live on in Japan today as a part of everyday life. The mindsets of our most admirable businessmen are pure Bushido. They act accountably, take personal responsibility, communicate clearly and honestly, uphold their honor, behave justly toward others, and work with unbounded energy.

"The big difference in these modern-day 21st century samurai and their ancestors is that today they serve their clients or customers, not fief lords. They are dedicated to maintaining their professional skills at the highest level, preserving their credibility and fulfilling their obligations to their employers as well as to society.

"Another difference between today's samurai businessmen and the warriors of the past is that they are at their best when they are free to make decisions based on their professional experience and skills."

Japan-resident Sam Jameson, foreign correspondent and former Japan bureau chief for *The Los Angeles Times* and *The Chicago Tribune*, and one of the few American journalists to become fluent in the Japanese language, suggests that anyone wanting to get an inkling of Bushido should see the Tom Cruise film, *The Last Samurai*.

"The attitudes and behavior of the samurai depicted in the film were fairly accurate; probably the most accurate representation of Bushido that has ever been put on film," Jameson said. "The skill, the courage, the stoicism and the idea of sacrifice depicted in the film became a part of the Japanese character during the samurai era. Some of these traits are still discernible in many areas of Japanese society today."

Jameson added that the ninja stunts in *The Last Samurai* were performed by members of a Tokyo group that earn their livelihood by giving performances of ninja skills. He also recalled a Sapporo Beer advertising slogan that he saw some time ago that was an example of the enduring samurai spirit. The slogan: *"Otoko ga damatte. Sapporo!"*—which may be translated as "A real man keeps quiet. And drinks Sapporo beer!"

Jameson said that the widespread social ethic of keeping a low profile, not making waves, keeping quiet about one's talents and not bragging about one's accomplishments could be traced to the samurai code.

The release of *The Last Samurai* film in Japan was quickly followed by CD renditions piled high in bookstores throughout the country.

2

The Spirit That Motivates the Japanese

Nihonjin no Seishin
(Nee-hone-jeen no Say-ee-sheen)

There are several dimensions to the character and spirit that have distinguished the Japanese since ancient times—most of which evolved directly from the samurai code of ethics, or were greatly enhanced by the code.

One of these dimensions is subsumed in the phrase *Ki ga susumanai* (Kee gah suu-suu-mah-nigh), which means, "My spirit is not satisfied".

This feeling of dissatisfaction, which over the centuries has been so powerful the Japanese could not ignore it, was the result of intense cultural conditioning to overcome whatever obstacles confronted them, and achieve whatever goals they set for themselves.

The origin of the *ki ga susumanai* feeling can no doubt be traced to the master-apprentice in the arts and crafts industries that were mainly imported from Korea and China from around the 6th century, and from a native Shinto impulse based on the demands of nature as a model.

Boys, apprenticed to masters when they were as young as seven or eight years old, were meticulously trained for ten to thirty or more years. One of the primary principles of this training was that the apprentices should never stop trying to improve their skills; that they should never be satisfied with their level of achievement.

In later centuries, this attitude became the bedrock of the samurai code of ethics. Inspired and guided by Zen principles, the warrior class became imbued with the concept that they could not give up no matter what the odds, and that they should never be satisfied with what they had achieved.

Still today this spirit of dissatisfaction is strong enough in most adult Japanese that it results in them going well beyond what might be described as "good enough," or as them having "done their duty". Traditionally, there has been no "done" or "good enough" in the Japanese mindset.

Obligation, Duty, Justice

Donald Westmore, Executive Director of the American Chamber of Commerce in Japan, has a very useful way of referring to the key words that encapsulate the most important of the values that underlie the spirit and much of the character of the Japanese. He refers to them as the "The Four G's"— *giri* (ghee-ree); *gisei* (ghee-say-ee), *gaman* (gah-mahn), and *gambaru* (gahm-bah-rue).

These four key words, plus a couple of derivatives, reveal the cultural values that motivate the Japanese and continue to make them a formidable people. Which of these key words is paramount depends on the circumstances at hand.

Giri means "obligation, duty, justice," and was the foundation of the samurai code of ethics, but it was an integral part of Japanese culture before the emergence of the samurai. In its more recent form, *giri* bound the people at birth to specific kinds and degrees of unending obligation to themselves, to their parents and siblings and to all others who touched their lives in a positive way—particularly teachers, employers, doctors, mentors, etc.

The power of *giri* has waned in today's Japan, but it still drives the Japanese to avoid shame, and to pay proper respect to seniors who are in positions of authority over them, real or perceived. *Giri* to one's name includes a deep sense of honor and pride, and, among the older generations a willingness to sacrifice their personal lives in the service of their employers.

Until the 1990s there was, perhaps, no more significant example of these cultural traits than the concept and practice of *chusei shin* (chuu-say-e sheen), which might be translated as "ultimate loyalty". The cultural demands on the Japanese to demonstrate *chusei shin* to classmates and to teammates at work and at play were enormous, often transcending what Westerners regarded as rational behavior. This trait has since waned considerably.

Another cultural trait that has remained a major element in the extraordinary spirit of the Japanese is expressed in the phrase *gaman kurabe* (gah-mahn kuu-rah-bay), which means "perseverance test" or "endurance match" between individuals or groups.

Japanese will often go into a *gaman kurabe* mode at the slightest hint of any kind of personal challenge, whether it is in eating, drinking, playing a game of baseball, or whatever. Japanese simply do not like to be outdone or lose at anything, and generally they will go to extremes to prevent that from happening.

Japanese businessmen, diplomats and politicians engaged in negotiations see the negotiating challenge as a *gaman kurabe*, and like their samurai and soldier ancestors, they commit themselves to endure and to persevere in the face of all odds. [Such "matches" often come down to who can drink more tea or coffee, sit longer, and say the least.]

Interestingly, Japanese do not necessarily like to engage in *gaman kurabe*. They do it because it is "the Japanese way," because they expect it of each other, and because generally no one is willing to break ranks and dispense with the custom.

In fact, foreigners going into negotiating sessions with Japanese can often win points by announcing up front that while they respect Japanese culture, they prefer not to engage in *gaman kurabe*, and respectfully recommend that everyone forego the custom.

Bearing the Unbearable

Another dimension of the traditional Japanese spirit is their willingness to bear the unbearable, or come very close to it, a trait that has been commonplace in Japan for centuries and institutionalized under the broad term *gamanzuyoi* (gah-mahn-zuu-yoe-ee), which includes the notions of "strong forbearance", "strong perseverance", "strong patience" and dedication to completing tasks.

Japan's traditional political and social systems, in which the rights of the government to stay in power and maintain peace took precedence over all human rights, made it imperative that the Japanese be extraordinarily patient, develop the ability to persevere against all odds, and suffer stoically in the process.

Gamanzuyoi could be called the glue of Japan's traditional culture, for it was what held Japanese society together, what made it work, and what was responsible for its greatest efforts, whether they succeeded or failed.

All of Japan's most famous arts, crafts and aesthetic practices, as well as its ideographic system of writing, required enormous amounts of *gamanzuyoi*. The accomplishments of Japan's samurai warriors and of its post-Shogunate soldiers were founded in *gamanzuyoi*.

In today's Japan, both the educational and the business management systems would disintegrate if it were not for the continuing willingness and ability of the Japanese to *gamanzuyoi*. And still today, when the Japanese are asked to make a list of their most distinctive, admirable and important character traits, *gamanzuyoi* is invariably somewhere near the top of the list.

This tradition of endurance and perseverance is still very much alive in Japan today, particularly among bureaucrats and older businessmen who see themselves as Japan's last bulwark of defense against the outside world.

But younger Japanese are becoming fed up with enduring the unendurable, and a growing number of voices can be heard saying they are not going to put up with it anymore. But as with so many of the other cultural traits of the Japanese, *gamanzuyoi* will remain a distinguishing characteristic of the Japanese for a long time, and will continue to be a factor in all of their international relationships.

Another cultural concept that is one of the foundations of the Japanese character and spirit is expressed in the germ *ganbaru* (gahn-bah-rue), which means to "hold out, to stand firm, to persist, to never give up". Its declarative and verb forms are, in fact, two of the most commonly used phrases in the vocabulary of the Japanese.

The Japanese are forever saying *ganbarimasu* (gahn-bah-ree-mahss), "I will persist; I will not give up"; *ganbarimasho* (gahn-bah-ree-mah-show), "let's persist; let's never give up"; and *ganbatte* (gahn-baht-tay), "hang in; don't give up."

What one might call the basic foundation of the Japanese character and spirit is subsumed in the word *gisei* (ghee-say-ee), which means "sacrifice". The Japanese have been conditioned since the beginning of their culture to sacrifice their individuality for the state, the community and the family—usually in that order.

In modern times, this sacrifice has primarily been to the company or organization for which the Japanese work—and has been manifested in the long working hours and diligence for which the Japanese have long been famous.

A full appreciation of the Japanese spirit and their way of doing business and engaging in other affairs requires an understanding of their cultural commitment to precise *do* (doh), or way of doing things (the *do* in Bushido), and to *kata* (kah-tah), which refers to patterns or forms of behavior

In pre-industrial Japan, the samurai and all other Japanese had specific *kata* for virtually everything they did, from the mundane actions of life to the most esoteric. There were *kata* for the martial arts, for drinking, eating, walking, speaking, and so on. These forms were precise and absolute, and because they were performed daily for generations they became an integral part of the mindset and physical behavior of the Japanese.

Younger Japanese are no longer conditioned in these *kata* from birth, and until they enter the adult world they are generally as individualistic and as untraditionally Japanese as typical Westerners. [To see glaring examples of the individualism of young Japanese today all you have to do is go to any of the dozens of entertainment and shopping districts in Tokyo and other cities that cater to the young and young at heart. Tokyo's Harajuku district is the weekend Mecca of Japan's young.]

But Japan's adult world is still a world of precise forms and processes that were honed to perfection during the age of the samurai, and both inwardly and outwardly the Bushido code continues to exercise significant control over the attitudes and behavior of individuals and groups.

This influence continues to be manifested in the use of the Japanese language, in bowing and in the conduct of the affairs in most offices in the country. It is also represented by such actions as the bold decision of Shigeyuki Kawata, CEO of the Sumida group of companies, to make English the official language of all employees in the corporate headquarters. [He gave the employees two years to make the switch from Japanese to English.]

There are, of course, a growing number of companies where there is no evidence of the more visible expressions of the samurai ethic. Most of these exceptions are new enterprises started by young computer and internet entrepreneurs who do not have to conform to the old *do* and *kata* because they created their companies from scratch, in their own image, and have deliberately chosen to ignore the traditional ways and forms.

What can the West learn about the spirit of the samurai? The emotional, intellectual and spiritual discipline that is necessary for a person to strive daily to do more, and do better, is lacking in most Westerners because it is not taught, either by example or in programmed instruction. But the potential is there, and the concept should be made an integral part of the educational system in non-Asian countries.

In Bushido literature, the lives of samurai were equated with cherry blossoms, a reference to the fact that the beautiful blossoms are so fragile that within a short time they are wafted away by the wind.

Interestingly, Tokyo-based business consultant Joe Schmelzeis, who was raised in Japan and is an authority on Bushido, equates the code and spirit of the samurai to the Boy Scouts. He says that the chapter headings in Inazo Nitobe's book, *BUSHIDO—The Soul of the Samurai*, sound very much like the Scout Law:

"A Scout is Trustworthy, Loyal, Helpful, Friendly, Courteous, Kind, Obedient, Cheerful, Thrifty, Brave, Clean, and Reverent." The Scout Motto is: "Be Prepared." The Scout Oath is: "On my honor, I will do my best, to do my duty to God and my country, and to obey the Scout Law; to help other people at all times, to keep myself physically strong, mentally awake, and morally straight".

"And finally, the Scout Slogan, "Do a good turn daily". A Westerner would find this a good maxim to follow in order to build up the balance in the "favor bank" in his reciprocity-based relationships with Japanese business associates."

When Schmelzeis became an Eagle Scout in Tokyo, his parents invited a number of notables, including the Emperor of Japan, and U.S. President Jimmy Carter to attend the family celebration. They didn't make it but Masaru Ibuka, the co-founder of Sony, did. He not only made it, he gave a speech in English, extolling the principles of the Boy Scouts, and congratulating Joe.

Said Schmelzeis: "The fact that Mr. Ibuka, who was the chairman of Sony at that time, took the time to come to my party was impressive enough, but that he had written and practiced a speech in English was an extraordinary demonstration of the traditional spirit of the samurai."

Joe's mother did get a telephone call from the Imperial Household, explaining that the Emperor couldn't make it, but wished the family the best.

3

Zen in the Japanese Mindset

Zen to Nihonjin no Shinsoushinri
(Zen toh Nee-hoan-jeen no Sheen-soh-uu-sheen-ree)

Japan's samurai warrior class, which came to power in the 12th century, became great advocates of Zen Buddhism the following century because the philosophy taught an austere life-style combined with an almost obsessive dedication to training in life skills and in the arts.

Since the lives of the samurai depended on extraordinary skill in the martial arts, and eventually an equally extraordinary degree of skill in a precise social etiquette, Zen became their spiritual guide as well as their training manual.

From the 13th century on, the samurai set the standards in every facet of Japanese life: in language and literature, in aesthetics, in the arts and crafts, in everyday behavior and in morality. The samurai also imbued Japanese culture with a strong martial nature that conditioned the Japanese to do things in a precise, regimented order and to abhor weakness or failure of any kind.

Still today there is no area of Japanese life that is not affected by the legacy of Zen, and there is still a significant Zen element in the character of every Japanese. Zen is still the heart of all of the martial arts for which Japan is famous, from aikido and karate to kendo; and the Zen rules that apply to learning these arts are taught as guidelines for success in business.

Nobuharu Yagyu, the 21st *iemoto* (ee-eh-moe-toe), or "head-master," of the Yagyu School of Kendo, explains that the secret to achieving skill in kendo is in the spirit that derives from repetition of *san ma no i* (sahn mah no ee), or "the three exercises."

The three exercises are receiving the right teaching, dedicating oneself to the teaching, and applying one's own ingenuity to what is learned from the teachings.

One of the key aspects of both absorbing and using the right teaching is emptying the mind of other matters, striving for complete detachment, and opening the mind fully in order to perceive completely and accurately whatever situation is at hand.

Yagyu says that it is essential that one nurtures *ken* (ken), "sight" and *kan* (kahn), "insight," in order to perceive reality and to be able to read an opponent's intentions—including the slightest movement or no movement at all—a lesson that applies to all human behavior, not just kendo.

The Compulsion to Improve

One of the primary Zen elements in the Bushido code is that one never totally masters anything and must therefore continually strive for improvement. This code has permeated Japanese culture for close to a thousand years, and had traditionally applied to everything they did. It is the foundation of the philosophy bound up in the expression *kaizen**¹ (kigh-zen), or "continuous improvement," which is one of the primary secrets of Japan's extraordinary accomplishments in all fields of endeavor.*

There is a well-known saying in Japanese that expresses the ongoing belief in continuous improvement: "Today I must beat the me of yesterday."

Hints that Western businesspeople must take up the study and practice of Zen if they want to compete effectively with the Japanese are not as ridiculous as they might seem. In fact, so much of the Japanese philosophy of business management is bound up in Zen concepts that it is impossible to discuss it, much less understand it, without bringing Zen into the picture.

The late Konosuke Matsushita, founder of one of the world's greatest industrial empires and considered the "god of management" by most Japanese, was a Zennist, pure and simple. He had no experience and no training or education whatsoever in business or management practices in the Western sense of these words. He also represented the best of the samurai code of ethics.*²

Until the 1990s, none of Japan's most successful businessmen owed any of their success to Western management practices. Their

---

*¹ I introduced the term *kaizen* to the Western business world in the early 1960s.

*² Matsushita Electrical Industrial Company began as a one-man shop in 1918, with Konosuke Matsushita repairing electrical appliances. A short time later, he began manufacturing bicycle lamp batteries. In 1929, by which time the number of employees had grown to 300, Matsushita announced the Basic Management Objectives of the company:

We dedicate ourselves to the development of the nation and to the development of our industry. In our endeavors, we hope to improve the quality of life around us. Profit alone will not be our principle goal; we will also search for ways to benefit society.

Matsushita said that this philosophy grew out of his realization that a private business was not a private matter; that a company did not work just for itself, but also for its dealers, its customers and the industry as a whole. In 1946, following the debacle of World War II, Matsushita restated the company's Basic Management Objective:

Recognizing our responsibilities as industrialists, we will devote ourselves to the progress and development of society and the well-being of people through our business activities, thereby enhancing the quality of life throughout the world.

successes [although often based on Western technology] were the result of applying traditional Japanese attitudes and patterns of behavior in organizing and managing people in the pursuit of common goals.

Many of the things Western businessmen have learned from Japan since the mid–1970s—from *kaizen* (kigh-zen) or "continuous improvement" to *nemawashi* (nay-mah-wah-she) or "behind the scenes consensus-building"—are rooted in Zen.

Whatever insights Western businessmen may have gleaned from reading the classic *Book of Five Rings*, written by Japan's most famous swordsman, Musashi Miyamoto (1584–1645), who was also a painter and calligrapher, were right out of a Zen primer.* [An English translation of this book became a bestseller in the U.S. after a writer for *Advertising* Age mentioned it in his column, saying it was one of the "manuals" that Japanese businessmen studied to improve their business skills.]

The modern-day painter-philosopher Riei Yamada (who has exactly the same "business" qualifications as Matsushita, Honda,

---

* It is recorded that Musashi Miyamoto killed over sixty samurai warriors in one-on-one duels before retiring, writing his book, and taking up painting. He was thirteen years old when he killed his first opponent in a duel—a much older samurai who was renowned for his skill with a sword. Like the moviedom "fast guns" of the American West, Miyamoto did not seek out opponents. Because of his reputation, they sought him out. He was noted for using psychology to distract and defeat his opponents, as well as a method he called "winning without fighting," which involved using a clever ruse to avoid fighting altogether. He killed one of the most famous swordsmen of his day, a fellow named Danryu, with a wooden sword. Danryu was so angry at Miyamoto showing up late for the fight [a serious slight], and bringing only a wooden sword [an even worse insult], that he charged furiously at Miyamoto, and was instantly struck down, his skull crushed.

Duels between Japan's samurai were, in fact, far less frequent than duels between politicians, businessmen and others in Europe and in the United States in the 18th and 19th centuries. Duels in New Orleans were so common in the 1800s that on one particular Sunday morning there were seventeen duels at the same dueling grounds. One of the most famous of the duels in early America occurred in 1804, when Aaron Burr killed Alexander Hamilton, one of the architects of the American government.

Sony's Morita and other renowned Japanese business founders), says that Japan's extraordinary economic success since 1945 is based on the influence of the Zen concept of *mu* (muu) in Japanese thinking and behavior.

The Selflessness Ideal

Mu means "emptiness", "selflessness" or the non-existence of self. Yamada claims that *mu* is the source of Japan's cultural character, and emphasizes that one must grasp the essence of this Zen concept in order to understand and deal with Japanese.

There is no denying that one of the fundamental problems encountered by Western businesspeople in their dealings with the Japanese derives from a fundamental difference in the way Westerners and traditional-minded Japanese view themselves in relation to others.

The Japanese were conditioned from ancient times to believe that being self-centered is one of the worst of all sins, and there have traditionally been numerous social, economic and political sanctions to encourage—and often enforce—group-centered attitudes and conduct.

From the last centuries of Japan's Heian era (784–1192), living the selfless life was held up as the ideal, and was referred to as *kokoro zukai* (koe-koe-roe zuu-kigh), which in poetic terms means something like "living by considering others from the heart."

This spiritual concept of a selfless life was a key component in the triad of Shinto*, Buddhist and Confucian philosophies that served as the building blocks of Japanese society, and was used by the early Imperial Courts as well as the following Shogunate governments as a primary theme in their political systems. Zen in particular taught that affluence was the enemy of character.

This is not to suggest that all Japanese, at any time, were in fact selfless, but a very significant proportion of the Japanese people—particularly until the 1960s—were unselfish to a remarkable degree, and played a key role in giving Japanese culture much of its special character.

On a human level, the idealized *kokoro zukai* life was one of the things that mitigated many of the harsher, often inhuman facets of Japan's feudal society, and enough of it remains today to now and then give a tantalizing glimpse of a better world.

In a business context, *kokoro zukai* represents the idealized relationship among employees, and between makers, subsidiaries, affiliated firms and the whole marketing/wholesaling/retailing network. Individuals making up the networks go to extreme lengths to protect and nurture these feelings, devoting their lives to maintaining the necessary relationships, with a diligence and dedication that, in the Western sense, goes beyond the call of duty.

In contrast to the Japanese way, Western culture conditions people to be self-centered in the sense that they look upon themselves as individuals, as completely separate entities, whose relationships with others are based on self-interest and self-preservation, with total independence being the ideal state.

This self-centered Western approach to life can be and often is sublimated to the interests of others, as in group sports and other types of team work, but these occasions are variations from the norm —and are a minor factor in the overall Western way of thinking and behaving, particularly in business.

---

* One of the reasons why Shinto became and remained so important in Japanese culture is that it celebrated the physical and sexual side of life with gusto. The primary essence of Shinto was physical cleanliness, spiritual purity and fertility. There was no direct connection with moral guilt. Good and evil were not fixed principles. They were relative, depending on the situation at hand. Shinto had no concept of original sin. Salvation was not something that occurred after death in a Heaven. It was sought and achieved in life by living in harmony with nature and the spirits. Foreigners visiting present-day Japan are fascinated by the frank and ribald display of sex-oriented fertility symbols (and behavior) at popular annual Shinto festivals.

One facet of the self-centeredness of Western businesspeople (mostly men) that used to shock the Japanese was the huge salaries many corporate executives pay themselves. This concept of "looking out for No. 1," often at the expense of others, was traditionally alien to the Japanese. But little by little this American morality has seeped into Japan's corporate culture.

While Zen was one of the cultural forces that played a key role in the Japanese attempts to create a perfectly selfless society, personally and in business, at least one aspect of its philosophy—its disdain for wealth—has virtually disappeared in Japan.

The First Zen MBA

Most attempts to explain how Japan could become an economic super power in less than thirty years, and why Japanese products went from being shoddy copies to the best in the world in ten years, have been incomplete. One reason for this failure is that the man who played a key role in this so-called miracle died in 1744.

Historically, there have been many examples of tiny nations and "city states" becoming super economic powers, so Japan is hardly unique in that respect. But the circumstances surrounding Japan's becoming the second largest economy on the globe are unique—and still a mystery to many.

This mystery is partially explained by the revolutionary teachings of a man named Baigan Ishida, who in later life took up the practice of Zen. Ishida was born in 1685 and died in 1744. Prior to his time, the economic philosophy that prevailed in Japan was based on an emphasis on diligence combined with frugality—concepts that are fundamentally opposed to each other. People were programmed to work hard but to live a very frugal life-style.

As the peaceful decades of the Tokugawa era passed, a well-to-do merchant class appeared, with some of the merchants becoming immensely wealthy. The government stepped in and began enforcing frugality laws, confiscating the entire business and estate of one of the oldest and wealthiest merchant families on a charge of "intolerable luxury."

This resulted in all other successful merchants assuming a low profile. The leaders of big merchant families like Mitsui created house rules that made it mandatory for members to avoid luxury, and concentrate on interpersonal relationships, loyalty to the family, and protecting their assets.

With the whole country ordered to reduce expenditures and consumption, the supply of goods went up while demand went down. The economy stopped growing, and the whole system went into a tailspin. By 1700, the country was experiencing a full-blown depression, which was made worse by a serious famine that lasted from 1716 to 1735.

A variety of solutions were attempted in an effort to bring the economy back into balance. One of these attempts involved resorting to metaphysical remedies that included workers taking time off to climb Mt. Fuji.

Then along came Baigan Ishida. Born into a strict farming family, Ishida was apprenticed to the owner of a dry goods shop in Kyoto when he was in his early teens. Under the apprentice system that existed at that time, apprentices became clerks when they were about twenty, and shop managers when they were thirty. They were not permitted to marry until they were forty. Most retired a few years later because the average lifespan at that time was fifty.

A few years after Ishida was apprenticed to the shop it went bankrupt, but he was too embarrassed to return home or tell his parents. When his parents came to Kyoto some time later to visit, they found him living in poverty.

Ishida went home with his parents, worked for a while as a

farmer, and was then apprenticed to another dry goods shop in Kyoto. Thus, instead of becoming a manager at thirty, the usual age, he was forty when he was promoted to that position.

During the course of his long apprenticeship, Ishida became a dedicated student of Zen, the ancient practice that taught mental control, how to distinguish between illusion and reality, diligence, austerity, simplicity and oneness with nature—goals that were achieved through meditation and work.

A Way of Developing Character

It occurred to Ishida that instead of working to accumulate material things and attempting to become wealthy, people should view work as a way of developing character. He retired shortly after being promoted to manager and opened a school to teach his new economic philosophy. No students enrolled so he started lecturing to people in the streets of Kyoto.

Ishida's teachings were summed up in the slogan *shogyo soku shugyo* (show-g'yoh soh-kuu shuu-g'yoh) which can be translated as "business (or work) is the pursuit of knowledge", or "work results in intuitive wisdom."

In more practical terms, Ishida's slogan meant that the primary purpose of work was to build character and virtue, not productivity. Ishida taught that frugality was honorable and one of the highest virtues, and that people should be judged by the content of their character, not their material possessions.

Since the economy was then burdened by production well in excess of the frugal lifestyle ordained by the government, Ishida's philosophy spread rapidly. Within a few years there were Ishida academies throughout the country.

Over the next several decades, Ishida's followers turned the concept of work from drudgery and an unwelcome necessity into a religious and philosophical experience. The more diligent the individual and the harder he or she worked, the greater the spiritual, emotional and intellectual satisfaction.

In 1932 Konosuke Matsushita, founder of Matsushita Electrical Industrial Corp., began to equate management with religion, and stated that business should be regarded as a sacred enterprise. He said that the mission of Matsushita was to enrich the life of every person on earth through material abundance, which was just as important as spiritual peace. He added that spiritual peace and material abundance were as inseparable as the two wheels of a cart.

Expounding on this theme in his autobiography, *Quest for Prosperity: The Life of a Japanese Industrialist* (PHP Institute), Matsushita wrote: "If the spiritual peace offered through the power of religion is added to a paradise of material abundance, human life will be complete. This is where the spirit of real business management lies…"

The more skilled the Japanese became in their work, and the greater the quality of the products they produced, the greater the satisfaction. This satisfaction-principle was another element encouraging the Japanese to strive for perfection in their efforts.

In this mindset, a product that functioned properly was not enough. It had to be refined and finished down to the last detail—everywhere; not just in the areas normally visible to the user. As time went by, Ishida's philosophy became the moral standard by which the Japanese measured themselves and others.

There were two other significant economic factors that were to have a profound influence on Japan, and still today play a major role in the country's economy, corporate philosophy and national politics. First was the relative scarcity of raw materials, and second was the over-abundance of labor.

This led the Japanese to become extraordinarily sensitive to the materials that went into their products, and to lavish labor on every product and project. From this era on, the quality of Japan's handicrafts rose higher and higher, to the level of art. It was this same approach, this same philosophy and dedication that the Japanese brought to the challenge of rebuilding Japan following the destruction suffered during World War II.

For the first decade following World War II, foreign importers controlled the quality of most products made in Japan. As soon as the Japanese were able to get out from under the influence of foreign buyers the quality of their goods began to rise, and by the early 1960s they were world leaders in many product categories.

The Japanese passion for detail and quality was to have a major impact on the United States. Not only were the Japanese able to capture large segments of the American market. When American manufacturers finally began trying to sell their merchandise in Japan, the majority of them failed because the overall quality and detailing of their products was far below Japanese standards and expectations.

It was to take American manufacturers some ten years before they were able to bring the quality of their products close to the level of the Japanese—a process that required them to create and implement a new corporate culture, some of which was copied from Japan.

Many Westerners, in all fields, unknowingly apply Zen precepts in their efforts to achieve success. They could benefit even more by familiarizing themselves with both the techniques and philosophical foundations of Zen.

One of the primary elements of Shinto incorporated into enterprise management following the industrialization of Japan (1870–1890) was the concept that management should follow the laws of nature, which create and control the destiny of all things. That is, things should be done according to natural processes. In practice, this meant a management system that took into account all of the traits of human beings, in combination with their natural hopes and desires for a peaceful, productive, happy life.

4

The Metaphysical Side of Job-Training

Jutsu to Shiteno Shokugyo Kunren
(Jute-sue toh Ssh-tay-no Show-kuu-g'yoh Koon-wren)

In the mid–1950s when I first began looking into the cultural and historical factors that fashioned the Japanese way of management, the thing that struck me the most powerfully was the metaphysical aspect of the thinking and training that went into the making of merchants and craftsmen in early Japan.

In the traditional Japanese way, the new carpenter's apprentice was not just put to work doing menial things and acting as servant to the master. He was also sent to the theater to learn about human relations and the role of things in the lives of people—a concept and practice that is unthinkable in a Western context.

Master carpenters also lectured their apprentices on the character and "spirit" of the wood used in the trade so that they would understand its nature and use it correctly. Apprentices were also taught to understand and respect the tools of the trade, caring for them as others would some treasured piece of art—just as the samurai glorified and sanctified their swords.

Samurai were programmed to treat their swords as sacred objects; as containing their soul. The making of a single sword followed precise Shinto rituals, and could take several months. They were the most valuable objects in the possession of ordinary samurai. Many swords became famous and were handed down for generations. Unlike most swordsmen, the samurai method of fighting did not involve striking the sword of an opponent with their own sword. The aim was to strike only the opponent, not his sword.

This very sophisticated approach to management and job-training occurred in the overall context of the culture, which emphasized team work, mutual responsibility, great sensitivity and respect for human relations, aesthetic appreciation, and the concept of continuous refinement in attitudes, personal behavior, skills and handiwork.

The formal educational system in Japan, with its emphasis on learning to read and draw the several thousand ideograms used to write the language, combined with a precise, finely structured etiquette and unquestioning obedience to authority, added to the built-in patterns of thought and behavior that made the Japanese good, easy-to-manage employees.

It was soon clear to me that it was this legacy of training and education that went far beyond the necessary practical knowledge and physical aspects of management and work that gave the Japanese way of doing things its distinctive flavor and special strengths.

It was also obvious why Japanese businessmen did not need any special courses in management to succeed in business. All they had to do was follow the dictates of the culture—their own instincts—in organizing, training and managing personnel. They knew naturally how to motivate other Japanese and how to inspire and maintain their loyalty.

These are attributes that are often lacking in American managers, in part because of the smorgasbord nature of American society. Another reason is that typical American youths are not taught to achieve beyond modest standards.

Proper habits must be ingrained in childhood—*samurai code of ethics*.

Another aspect of the metaphysical side of samurai-type business management that does not appear to be significant in the thinking of most Western businessmen is that if a company fails to make a profit it is because it is not fulfilling enough of the fundamental mission of an enterprise, which is to contribute to society. Konosuke Matsushita referred to this factor as co-existence and co-prosperity.

Japan's famous product after-service also has a metaphysical element that is dramatically illustrated in the management philosophy of Matsushita. He said that manufacturers should look upon their products as their children—specifically as married daughters who are sent out into the world but should not be forgotten and that there should be regular follow-up to make sure they were doing well.

The Japanese attention to product details is well known. Those following the way of the samurai also extend this attention to detail across the board in all of their business and professional affairs. A president or chairman of the board escorting departing visitors to the elevator and sometimes to the front door is obeying one of the fundamental tenets of the samurai code. Treating every visitor, including those who have come to complain, as an honored guest is the samurai way.

These are common sense aspects of behavior that many in the West ignore as being unnecessary and/or a waste of time. They are neither. They are an important human element in the conduct of business.

5

Power of the Right Mental Attitude

Tadashii Kangaekata no Pawaa
(Tah-dah-she-ee Kahn-guy-kah-tah no Pah-wah)

The goal in the making of a samurai was to unite the body and mind or spirit to the point that there was no difference between thinking something and doing it. This state was called *mushin* (muu-sheen), or *munen* (muu-nane), meaning "no mind"—that is, the mind has been rendered blank so that it does not interfere with the actions of the body. This state may also be called *muga* (muu-gah), which is defined as without ego or a state of ecstasy.

In more practical terms, achieving a state of mushin, or getting as close to it as possible, is the goal of the martial arts as well as the creation of fine arts.

Adds Japan educated journalist-author Glenn Davis: "Thinking of nothing is an art, not a science. Arts can be taught, so using Bushido "mind clearing" techniques could increase the effectiveness of businesspeople as well as people in general."

All of the training of the samurai was designed to achieve *mushin*, at which point they could achieve perfection in any action taken, whether with the sword, the bow, or any other weapon. This training began with the physical side, and then proceeded to the mental and spiritual aspects of all actions.

Training with the sword began at an early age. In most samurai families, this training was well underway by the time boys were seven. It was not approached as a game. It was deadly serious. Next came training with other weapons and in the art of jujitsu.

In addition to training the body and mind in these physical skills, the training of samurai youths included teaching them to have no fear, to suppress all sentimental feelings when it came to fighting, and to be aggressive and spontaneous in making decisions and taking action.

The mental and spiritual side of the training of samurai youths included meditation and subjecting them to such hardships as going without food, being exposed to frigid weather, and becoming hardened to pain.

At the age of fifteen, youths became men, and from that day on they were required to wear two swords, a long one to use on others, and a short one to use on themselves when suicide was in order. The Bushido code required them to carry these weapons at all times when they were in public, and most generally wore them indoors as well, taking them off only when sleeping, and, in certain circumstances, when sitting on the floor. [As noted earlier, when samurai youths reached the age of fifteen, one part of the training of some of them was beheading convicted felons.]

In present-day Japan not many people strive to achieve a state of *mushin*, but having the right attitude is still on top of the list of traits that the Japanese most admire. The main job of master teachers is to impart the correct attitude to students and novices.

> It is difficult to defeat enemies; it is easy to defeat one's self—*samurai code of ethics.*

Burning With Ambition

The motivation that was programmed into the samurai for centuries is still visible in Japan today. Most Japanese still "burn" with ambition, and are motivated well beyond what is common in the West. This motivation has long been described by the word *moretsu* (moh-rate-sue), which means "fierce, furious," and refers to the attitude of these Japanese in their approach to training and working.

Japanese manufacturers teach their sales people that sales without service is not sales; and even though providing service virtually without limit may be exhausting and sometimes thankless, it should be done joyfully because it represents the heart of the maker.

Matsushita appears to have pioneered the idea of sending new employees to work for several months in shops carrying the company's products in order for them to meet customers face-to-face on a daily basis, listening to their complaints, needs and recommendations. The insights they gain are one of the strengths of Japanese companies.

Secret of the Martial Arts

Westerners who have become involved in such martial arts as aikido, judo or kendo know that form alone, no matter how perfect, is not enough to produce a winner. They learn that without the proper *kokorogamae* (koh-koh-roh-gah-my), "mental attitude, readiness, preparation," they do not stand a chance when facing an opponent who has mastered both *kamae* (kah-my), attitude and form.

Attitude is the thing that gives extraordinary power to noh and kabuki actors. With attitude alone, master kabuki and noh actors can express virtually every human emotion known, and with one or two steps or a hand gesture, create an illusion of action that is so powerful the audience is swept up in the drama.

During Japan's long samurai period when skill with a sword was often a matter of life or death, the greatest masters of the sword were those who first learned the right attitude. It was said that a master swordsman could instantly judge the skill of an opponent by his attitude—before the opponent made the first move.

The face of the master swordsman was said to have been like the frozen expression of a noh mask—saying nothing and yet saying everything at the same time—an expression that one still sees today in middle-aged and older Japanese men.

When Japanese corporations interview job applicants, the first thing they measure and judge in the candidates is their *kokorogamae*. If they do not have the "right attitude," they will generally not be hired, regardless of how brilliant the candidates might be or how many skills they may have developed.

In promoting employees, Japanese companies rate attitude above virtually everything else. Their philosophy is that the higher people go up the managerial ladder, the more vital it is for them to have the right attitude.

In the Japanese context of things, the right attitude for a corporate employee includes such things as being a good listener, and being humble, polite, observant, cooperative, diligent and determined, and [until recently] not openly aggressive. Any analysis of Japanese character and behavior in planning and implementing projects, in interacting with co-workers, clients, and customers, and in the way they perform their work invariably begins and ends with an evaluation of their *kokorogamae*.

Traditionally, the "right attitude" was programmed into all

Japanese by the culture. It was something that the Japanese absorbed as they grew up, because the whole culture was based on precisely identified attitudes that had long since become second nature.

When Japanese businesspeople meet their foreign counterparts for the first time, the judgment they make about whether or not they want to pursue the relationship often hinges on what they read in the attitude of the foreigners.

Western golfers, bowlers, tennis players and other professional sportspeople learn very quickly that if they do not have the right attitude, they cannot become champions. But most Westerners do not knowingly and deliberately make use of this knowledge in their daily lives.

This is one of the reasons why most foreigners are generally at a disadvantage when dealing with the Japanese—when the Japanese are in groups—because the mental attitude of the Japanese often gives them unassailable power.

Another factor in the creation of Japanese employees with the right attitude is subsumed in the word *shikitari* (she-kee-tah-ree), which means "how things are done." *Shikitari* incorporates all of the values, standards and rituals that make up the prevailing beliefs and behavior in a particular Japanese company. These features differ to some degree from company to company because they are primarily the creation of the executives running the companies; nevertheless, the features of the *shikitari* of a company are all rooted in the culture of Japan and are therefore similar.

Generally speaking, the *shikitari* of a company are not written down and are not explicitly taught to new employees. The *shikitari* are things that newcomers are expected to absorb by osmosis, by listening, watching, imitating, and only rarely by asking questions during their first years with the company.

Because so many of the *shikitari* of a company are subtle and often invisible to the outsider, foreigners who work for Japanese companies typically find themselves working blindly. They often do not know what they are supposed to do, or how they are supposed to act. The result is that they tend to be in a constant state of uncertainty and frustration.

Within a company in which everyone knows and abides by *shikitari*, it is taken for granted that everyone understands and appreciates what everyone else is doing, and that there will be little or no disagreement because compromise and cooperation are built into the system.

In a purely Japanese context, *shikitari* binds the company into a highly directed, highly drilled team that is formidable when it plays against other teams, including foreign companies which are not so tightly structured or focused in their behavior.

Poetry also played an important role in the Japanese having the right mental attitude, especially during trying times. The custom of writing poetry was imported from Korea and China around the 7th century, and by the 9th century had become a primary ingredient in the culture of upper-class Japanese, particularly in the Imperial Court in Kyoto, where it became the favorite way of communicating among the lords and ladies. From there it spread to the fief lords and their retainers, and finally to the common people.

The samurai class, which rose from the 12th century, naturally adopted the custom of writing poetry, and used it extensively to compose their minds, refine their thinking process, strengthen their aesthetic appreciation and express their deepest philosophical thoughts.

Says Mutsuo Shukuya, educator and *tanka* poet master, "The role that poetry played in the lives of the samurai, and later in the lives of virtually all Japanese, was extraordinary, and I believe, unprecedented in any other country."

One of the most famous incidents of the role that poetry has played in Japan, recounted by Shukuya, involved the famous forty-seven *ronin* (roh-neen) or masterless warriors, who avenged the unjustified death of their young lord by killing the Shogunate official who brought about his untimely end, and then committed ritual suicide when ordered to do so by the Shogunate government.

The message the leader of the forty-seven ronin sent to his informant in Edo (Tokyo) to find out when the official was going to be in his private residence and thus vulnerable to attack, along with the reply he received, were in the form of poems whose meaning was innocuous to others.

During the samurai era, the right mental attitude included having respect for authority and the laws. Those who failed in this were subject to harsh treatment. The official description of a robber's execution would deter most people from crime. First, all of the hair on his body was burned off and his fingernails were pulled out. Then the tendons that controlled his feet were cut and holes were bored into his body with drills. Finally his back was broken and he was boiled in soy sauce. Executions were public, and people were required to witness them as a deterrent to misbehavior and crime.

Says Shukuya: "Composing *haiku* or *tanka* poetry concentrates the mind, sensitizes the individual to the beauty and nuances of nature, improves the ability to see and feel the essence of both material and immaterial things, and soothes the spirit."

Another aspect of Japanese behavior that was inspired by Bushido is for employees to behave as if they were the founders and owners of the enterprises, and thus give their all to help make them successful—an ethic traditionally supported by the Confucian-oriented family nature of Japanese management.

While this ethic has lost much of its power since the 1990s, it remains a significant part of the cultural character of most Japanese employees (even though they don't own stock in the companies), providing corporations with an energy source that goes beyond what is common in the West.

Still another element of the samurai-inspired mental attitude that is expected of the Japanese, in business, in sports or in whatever, is that they will automatically strive at all times *to do better than their best*.

This attitude is, in fact, built into the phrase *isshokenmei yari-masu* (ees-show-kane-may-ee yah-ree-mahss) that one constantly hears. It is usually said and translated to mean "I will do my best", but the deeper meaning is that "I will stake my life" on accomplishing whatever task is at hand. When one's life is at stake, one can perform above what is normal for people.

In such companies as Matsushita, the mental attitude of employees is not left to chance, or to what the employees bring with them when they become employees. These companies follow a set of four principles in creating the mental attitude they want their employees to have.

These four principles are: (1) to have a basic business philosophy that provides a clear reason for the existence of the enterprise, along with management practices to fulfill this philosophy; (2) the precepts of the company philosophy must be ingrained in the minds of the employees to the point that they will instinctively behave according to the precepts; (3) that employees must be trained to work without constant oversight, have a strong sense of responsibility and be creative in their approach to everything they do; and (4) that all employees be trained to develop a sense of social responsibility.

Staying Hungry

Another facet of the right mental attitude expected of Japanese employees has been described as "staying hungry"—that is, never being satisfied with design, quality, productivity, sales or service, and being obsessed with the need to do more things and to do them better.

This characteristic, too, is a product of Zen and Bushido, and while it is still visible in the employees of Japan's leading manufacturers, it has diminished dramatically in the cultural programming of the younger generations.

However, as the younger Japanese reach adulthood and join the corporate world they are under extraordinary pressure, directly and indirectly, to adopt the patterns of thought and behavior that still prevail in the corporations, with the result that fundamental changes in the culture are much slower than what might be expected by outsiders. From day one, new recruits are expected to demonstrate the same qualities of diligence and self-motivation as older employees, and for the most part, they do.

While most Americans and other Westerners are aware that a positive mental attitude is crucial to good health and achieving goals, only a small percentage of the people routinely apply this principle to their lives.

As in traditional Japan, the programmed instilling of a positive mental attitude should be made an integral part of all cultures.

6

The Emotional Foundation
of Japanese Behavior

Bijinesu no Kanjoteki Kiban
(Bee-jee-nay-sue no Kahn-joh-tay-kee Kee-bahn)

In feudal Japan, the highest morality was fulfilling personal obligations and conforming to a precise etiquette that controlled every aspect of behavior. In this kind of society, a person's morality was visible! It was manifested constantly through one's speech and whether or not one followed the precisely programmed etiquette in interacting with others.

Under the watchful eyes of the samurai warrior ruling class, the standards of etiquette became higher and higher, and the punishment for misbehavior became sure, swift and often fatal. This combination of factors resulted in the Japanese becoming extremely demanding and emotional in their expectations from others, and made them equally sensitive to the feelings and needs of others.

However, according to Dr. Tadanobu Tsunoda, Japan's premiere otology and audiology authority and author of *The Japanese Brain* and numerous other publications on the subject, there is more to the emotional factor in the makeup of the Japanese than these cultural explanations.

Dr. Tsunoda says that the Japanese are programmed by their language to be unusually emotional while all other people [except for Polynesians] are programmed by their languages to be more analytical. He explains that the extraordinary number and use of vowels in the Japanese and Polynesian languages results in these languages being processed by the right side of the brain—the emotional side—while English and all other languages are processed on the left side of the brain.

He characterizes the Japanese brain as inharmonic (which includes most of the sounds of nature), and non-Japanese brains as harmonic (which includes sounds created by someone to be harmonic, such as Western music).

Dr. Tsunoda says that when the Japanese are in their normal environment, the right side of the brain is generally dominant, and that in other people, the left side of the brain is generally dominant. He says this language-based hard wiring of the brain is complete by the time a person is nine years old, and that the brains of Japanese born and raised in non-Japanese speaking environments are the same as other non-Japanese, proving that it is the Japanese language that creates the differences in the thinking and behavioral patterns of the Japanese and foreigners.

[I have often heard Japanese complain that listening to and speaking English for extended periods of time is especially tiring—apparently because it requires the use of the left side of their brains, which would seem to prove Dr. Tsunoda's theory.]

Dr. Tsunoda's theories on how the brain processes languages led him to invent an electronic "key tapping" system to determine which side of the brain is dominant, and he has since tested hundreds of people, including me, from many different language backgrounds. I thought my fairly early exposure to the Japanese language might make me different. It didn't.

It has, of course, been well documented that the Japanese are exceptionally emotional in their reaction to nature and to human relationships. However, I have noted numerous times in the past that when Japanese who are fairly fluent in English speak in English their mindset and behavior also changes. This would also seem to bear out Dr. Tsunoda's theory, and it is something that many foreigners in Japan quickly pick up on, and try to use to gain an advantage.

This phenomenon can be a trap, however, particularly in business and diplomatic situations, and especially if the dialogue at hand involves just one Japanese. First, there is a tendency for the Japanese to regard what is said in English as unofficial and not necessarily binding. And second, except in rare cases, an individual cannot bind his co-workers or company to a commitment he makes on his own.

Nurturing Emotional Needs

One of the Japanese solutions to the problem of making their emotion-oriented society work was the development of the philosophy of *kikubari* (kee-kuu-bah-ree)—that is, paying special attention to the emotional as well as to the practical aspects of life.

Konosuke Matsushita, founder of the giant Matsushita conglomerate, was one of the most famous believers in the virtue and value of *kikubari*. One of Matsushita's rules was that every need and expectation of a customer should be anticipated, and that any customer who was dissatisfied with a product for any reason should be treated with even more consideration and politeness than when he or she bought the product.

Kikubari in its traditional state does not allow for halfway measures. As practiced and taught by the Japanese, it means that the seller or provider must go all the way to make sure that the customer is not only satisfied but feels good.

While the importance of *kikubari* is gradually decreasing in Japan because of cultural dilution and economic changes, enough of it remains to make it an essential ingredient in achieving success in Japan in any field.

Taking Care of Feelings

Another of the key factors in the personal and emotional element in dealing with the Japanese business and in personal affairs is expressed in the term *kimochi* (kee-moe-chee), which means "feelings." In short, *kimochi* or "feelings" must be satisfied first before a business relationship can begin with a Japanese company, and the good feelings must be sustained thereafter in order for the relationship to continue on a mutually acceptable basis.

The Japanese are not adverse to facts and figures. In fact, they typically go overboard in accumulating data. But their final decision in matters at hand is often based more on *kimochi* than on hard data—a circumstance that foreign businesspeople and politicians often find mystifying and frustrating.

Successfully negotiating a business relationship with a Japanese company does not end the need for investing *kimochi* in the relationship. In fact, it often becomes even more critical, because after the courtship and honeymoon are over, differences in perceptions, opinions, approaches and requirements invariably surface, requiring that the two sides remain in a constant state of adjusting the relationship.

If the *kimochi* ties between all of the key individuals involved on both sides is not strong enough to withstand all of the pushing and pulling that normally occurs, the relationship will be an unpleasant one and may be short-lived.

On the private side of life in Japan, *kimochi* actions are not always quid pro quo. People routinely do favors for others as expressions of friendship and goodwill and without expecting anything in return. When people feel embarrassed or put in an awkward position by a gift or favor, all the giver has to do to put them at ease is to say, *Kimochi desu* (Kee-moe-chee dess), or "It's feeling."

Not surprisingly, doing business successfully in Japan requires an extraordinary emotional investment, which by Western standards is often to the extreme. By the same token, there is reason to believe that the typical corporate culture in the United States has been, and still is to a significant degree, lacking in the emotional department.

Until the latter decades of the 20th century, the prevailing business culture in America appears to have been based on keeping emotion out of the corporate world. This culture did not start to change significantly until competition from Japan began to threaten the existence of many American industries.

Human needs, as expressed in emotions and feelings, are still not fully addressed by most American corporations, and the Japanese themselves are now under serious pressure to de-emotionalize their traditional corporate culture. A new human-oriented economic paradigm is needed.

Washing Away Sins

It is generally accepted that confession is good for the soul, and Christianity has gone so far as to make the admission of sins a prerequisite for enjoying the blessings of the Church and the assurance of reservations in heaven.

Western justice, however, has never been as lenient as Japanese justice in its treatment of people who confess to wrongdoing. On the contrary, law enforcement agencies in the West put a great deal of effort into getting people to confess to crimes in order to justify punishing them. In pagan Japan on the other hand, the treatment of people who confess to unlawful activity has been much more Christian.

A confession and an expression of regret have traditionally been accepted in Japan as satisfying some of the demands of society for the punishment of miscreants. This irony can probably be traced to the differences between Japanese gods and the God of Christianity. Japanese gods have traditionally been rather human in their behavior, suffering from many of the weaknesses of us mortals. No doubt as a result of their human characteristics, Japanese gods have been more generous and forgiving in their attitudes toward human transgressions.

The primary requirement of Japanese gods is that people guilty of misbehavior or of failure to fulfill their obligations must demonstrate *hansei* (hahn-say-ee), or "self-reflection." In Japanese philosophy, it is assumed that sincere *hansei* will result in the recognition of guilt and the resolve to do better in the future. This presumption indicates that the Japanese opinion of humanity is significantly higher than what exists in most Western cultures.

Hansei has long been institutionalized more or less across the board in Japanese society—in interpersonal relationships, in the justice system, and in the business community as well. If an individual in a company makes a mistake, he or she is generally not singled out for some kind of sanction. Instead, a group effort is made to find out why the mistake was made, and to institute changes in the system that will preclude such mistakes in the future.

However, managers and executives who continue to make mistakes are invariably called upon by their employees and/or the public to *hansei*, and correct their thinking and their behavior.

Groups of Japanese frequently come together in *hansei kai* (hahn-say-ee kie), or "self-reflection meetings", in an effort to find out what they are doing wrong, or to improve on their success by reflecting on their way of thinking and doing things.

Foreign businessmen, politicians, and diplomats who are dealing with Japan and want to bring about substantive changes in a relationship might do well to approach the challenge in the form of *hansei kai*—something that the Japanese fully understand and appreciate.

If a person is unfortunate enough to be accused of wrongdoing by the Japanese, the first and most important thing to do is to apologize, even if there is no guilt—in which case the apology is for becoming involved in the situation, rather than confessing guilt.

If a person is guilty, in any sense and to any degree, it is wise for the person to announce that he or she will engage in self-reflection, or *hansei shimasu* (hahn-say-ee she-mahss). This promise of self-rehabilitation generally results in a lesser degree of punishment, and is something that could be used more often in the justice systems of the West.

7

The Indulgent-Love Way of Doing Business

Bijinesu Youshiki ni miru Amae no Kouzou
(Bee-jee-nay-sue Yoh-she-kee nee me-rue
Ah-my no Koh-Zoh)

One of the most powerful facets of Japan's traditional culture is a concept known as *amae* (ah-my), which evolved from the ancient Shinto imperative for mutual dependence based on peaceful, harmonious co-existence with others and with nature.

Amae may be translated as "indulgent love," and refers to the ideal relationship between humans, meaning that all relationships should be based on absolute, unrestricted love that includes magnanimously accepting the faults and mistakes of others, and allowing them to impose upon your goodwill.

Presented as the ideal philosophy for human relations, *amae* required that people repress all selfish instincts and behave toward each other as mothers do to beloved children—treating them generously and kindly, regardless of their behavior.

In this idealized world, people could have absolute faith that they would not be cheated, disadvantaged or embarrassed by anyone, in any way. *Amae* incorporated the concepts of absolute dependence and trust in all human relations.

Of course, this high ideal was never fully realized, but it had enough influence on the character and behavior of the Japanese that it made them among the most honest, kindest and helpful people in any society, before or since.*

Amae was already the basic foundation of Japanese thought and behavior long before the appearance of the samurai. In effect, the samurai regarded themselves as the "parents" or guardians of the common people, but there was a catch to their "love." Theirs was a stern love that demanded absolute obedience to the etiquette and moral guidelines set down by the Bushido code of behavior.

As interpreted by the samurai, *amae* required exercising extraordinary restraint (*enryo* / en-rio) in both speech and manner, fulfilling all social obligations (*giri* / ghee-ree), and avoiding (*haji* / hah-jee) shame—shaming oneself as well as shaming others.

The *amae* factor remains readily discernible in Japan today, especially in the business world where stable, supporting relationships are especially important. The use of *amae* is also obvious among politicians whose success and careers are built on personal relationships, but it is not as obvious as it is in the public sector, since politicians have so much to hide.

Businesspeople, both consciously and subconsciously, want and need *amae* relationships with everyone with whom they do business, so much of their initial effort in establishing business relationships with others is designed to create *amae*. The reason, naturally

---

* Since the early decades of the Tokugawa Shogunate (1603–1868), the honesty of the average Japanese has been incredible when compared with that of the average Westerner. Individuals (including taxi drivers!) still today go to extreme lengths to return lost items to their owners, often at considerable expense to themselves.

enough, is the desire to avoid problems and the possibility of failure.

It naturally takes longer for the Japanese to develop an *amae* relationship with foreigners than it does with other Japanese, but it is not as difficult as it might first seem if one knows the steps and rules involved.

The process of building an *amae* relationship is simply enough. It involves eating and drinking together, exchanging gifts and other tokens of friendship and obligation, and participating in the various passages of life, such as attending weddings, funerals, graduations and the like.

Protecting Business Relationships

Rifts in business relationships between Westerners and Japanese often occur because the Western side is not aware of or does not understand the concept of *amae*. One of the key aspects of this cultural trait is that you will not do anything to upset the harmony of the relationship, even if it means you must accept some kind of disadvantage. Westerns often find this part of the relationship both surprising and difficult to deal with.

In the Japanese mind-set the relationship is more important than its parts, and keeping it on an even keel takes precedence over occasional disturbances.

Without advance knowledge, there are numerous manifestations of *amae* in action that Westerners regard as unreasonable if not irrational or just plain bad business. They are looking at the situation with a narrow focus. The Japanese view tends to be wide-angled, holistic and endless.

As actually practiced by most adults today, especially in business, *amae* generally consists of imposing on the goodwill of others on the assumption that such behavior is understood as being reciprocal.

Says Tokyo-based consultant Joe Schmelzeis, a Harvard Business School graduate who went through elementary, junior and senior high school in Japan and is bilingual and bicultural: "*Amae* requires that you honor unreasonable requests or disruptive behavior from your business associates because it is a give-and-take relationship. This wins you points that you can collect on when something comes up that you want."

While virtually the whole web of traditional Japanese morality was designed to encourage and enforce harmony, it was a hierarchical harmony based on the political imperatives of those in power, rather than serving the individual needs and aspirations of the people at large.

Harmony was, in fact, a tool used by those in power to exercise political, economic and spiritual control over all levels of Japanese society. In this context, it was given precedence over the welfare of the people.

By demanding virtually absolute harmony, the samurai code resulted in behavior that was often diametrically opposed to human instincts and needs, and in this respect was antihuman. The ritual of ceremonial suicide by cutting open one's stomach was one of the more bizarre examples of the code's requirements.*

The Japanese way of sustaining and developing business relationships, based on the concept of *amae* and other cultural imperatives, is to stay constantly engaged with meetings and dialogues— which often take place after hours in bars, cabarets, lounges, restaurants, etc. [See: *Using the "Water Business."*]

---

* The stomach was believed to be the seat of the spirit/soul. This, it is said, led to the development of *harakiri* (hah-rah-kee-ree) or "cutting the stomach" as the samurai way of suicide. The fact that it was extremely painful and physically difficult to do was regarded as a demonstration of the courage and resolve that was a key part of the character of the samurai.

8

The Power of Paternalism

Osorubeki Onjo-shugi
(Oh-soh-rue-bay-kee Own-joh-shuu-ghee)

One of the major tenets of the Bushido code was Japanese-style paternalism. The samurai looked upon themselves as the "parents" of common people, serving as role models for them and responsible for seeing that they behaved in the expected manner—that is, according to rules established by the samurai.

But this attitude toward common people was not expressed in terms of paternalism in the Western sense. It was seen as, and described as, *onjo-shugi* (own-joe shuu-ghee) or "humanism," which in the Japanese context goes well beyond what paternalism means.

Until the rupture of Japan's "bubble economy" in 1990–1, *onjo-shugi* was a major ingredient in employer-employee relationships in Japan. It was much stronger in some companies than in others, but all company-employee relationships were based on humanistic as well as pure economic principles.

The Importance of "Warm Feelings"

Onjo by itself means "warm feelings" in the sense of the feelings that loving parents have for their young children; *shugi* is the "ism" part of humanism. Idemitsu Oil Company was long held up as the ultimate in *onjo-shugi*, but there were thousands of other lesser known companies that followed the ancient code just as religiously.

Onjo-shugi has taken a beating since the early 1990s, but the principle is still alive and cannot be ignored in managing companies in Japan. Most employees still do not view themselves as just selling a certain number of hours of their time per day or week. They identify themselves with their companies to a degree that goes beyond what is common in the West. In some companies this identification takes on the coloring of a vested ownership interest.

Foreign businesspeople operating businesses in Japan are well advised to be aware of the ongoing role on *onjo-shugi* in their employee contracts and management policies, and make sure they follow through on the personal obligations that are part of the relationship—which often includes arranging marriages.

Without these "warm feelings" between managers and employees, working with Japanese can be very uncomfortable and frustrating for foreigners.

There are examples of employers in the West who treat their employees kindly and warmly, much as if they were family members, but they are rare. The concept appears to be incompatible with the prevailing corporate culture.

It does seem, however, that the trend in the United States is toward a more human-oriented business culture, providing a more fertile ground for the adoption of *onjo-shugi* as a cultural standard.

In 1922, when tiny Matsushita Electric Industrial Company was three years old, Konosuke Matsushita and his wife, Mumeno, took several young employees into their household, where they were clothed, fed, and trained as if they were members of the family. This continued until 1934, when Matsushita opened a "factory school" that trained thirteen-and-fourteen-year olds for five years before they went to work in one of his factories. The training consisted of four hours a day of academic instruction and four hours of vocational training, six days a week.

9

Taking the Best and Leaving the Rest

Shusha Sentaku no "Myou"
(Shuu-shah Sen-tah-kuu no M'yoh)

Prior to the end of Japan's feudal social system in 1945–6 and the introduction of democracy, the Japanese utilized a highly honed sense of discrimination in what they imported into the country. By the time Chinese arts, crafts and other learning began to arrive in Japan in the 6th and 7th centuries, the Japanese already had a well-established sense of self and a cultural core of Japaneseness that was virtually impervious to outside influences.

This core of Japaneseness made it possible for the Japanese to import waves of technology, philosophy and ethics from China and Korea and change them to fit their own predetermined mindset.

This process, which was to continue throughout Japan's history, is now referred to as *ii toko dori* (ee toh-koh doh-ree) or as "picking the best part." Early Japanese not only had the ability to pick the best part of the technology, knowledge and value systems they imported, they were generally capable of improving on them.

This same cultural skill played a key role in the creation of the Bushido code from elements of Shinto, Buddhism, Confucianism, Mencianism and Zen. Despite Bushido's shortcomings, this ability to screen things with a discerning eye, extract the best parts and make the results better, was a major factor in Japan's becoming an economic super power, with examples abounding in virtually every technological field and industry in the country.

Foreign businesspeople finally began picking up on this Japanese talent around 1970, and since then have benefited in many ways from cooperating in the development of technology and products. Foreign businesses should pursue more joint efforts with their Japanese counterparts to take advantage of their special expertise.*

---

* *New York Times* columnist Thomas L. Friedman made an astute and vitally important observation in contrasting the highly successful cultures of Japan, Korea, Taiwan and Singapore with the Arab countries that are still in the feudal age. He noted that the success of the above-named resource-poor Asian countries was based on the fact that they assessed their weaknesses then took the rational and human approach. They educated their citizens, learned as much as possible from advanced nations of the West, and dedicated themselves to competing with those nations on their terms.

10
Failure is Not an Option

Shippai wa Yurusarenai
(Sheep-pie wah Yuu-ruu-sah-ray-nigh)

The samurai code of ethics by which the Japanese lived for so long did not condone failure of any kind, anywhere or any time. Where the samurai themselves were concerned, failure to fulfill all of their obligations to their lords was not only inexcusable, it was regarded as a capital offense, requiring them to take their own lives.

As the generations passed, a relatively less demanding version of the samurai code of honor, which included avoiding failure at virtually any cost, gradually seeped into the culture of the common people. They were not required to commit suicide to wipe out the shame of personal failures in life or in business, but they did face death, often immediate, if they failed to pay proper respect to the samurai, particularly to samurai lords.

In addition to the importance of proper behavior in their personal manners, the Japanese for centuries were also conditioned to strive for perfection in their work, and to avoid making mistakes of any kind. *Ippo machigaru to!* (eep-poh mah-chee-gow toh), or "just one mistake…!," could be devastating.

Still today, fear of making a mistake or failing remains an important factor in the personal as well as professional lives of the Japanese. While failure in business is no longer officially or socially viewed as either life or career threatening, because of the need for entrepreneurs and risk-taking in order to keep up with the rest of the world, it is still unofficially regarded as a serious setback.

On the positive side, the Japanese fear of making mistakes has resulted in them striving far beyond what most Westerners regard as normal to perfect their skills, to accomplish their work, and to win in any kind of competition.

Building on the Failure Taboo

In fact, virtually all of the positive traits for which the Japanese are known today are enhanced by their deep-seated compulsion to avoid failure and to get as close to perfection as possible in anything they set out to do.

Westerners do not have to be taught anything about failure or risk-taking, but there is a lesson to be learned from the Japanese in the diligence and energy with which they approach tasks of whatever kind. For one, their on-the-job demeanor is in stark contrast to what one typically sees in the U.S. and elsewhere.

Some time ago, an American retail executive visiting Japan asked me to accompany him on a visit to the Ginza branch of the Mitsukoshi Department Store in downtown Tokyo—something that I had suggested he do. After touring several floors, the executive turned to me and said: "Now I know why the Japanese are so successful!"

He was referring to the way the managers and staff behaved from the moment customers entered the store.

11

The New Business Mantra

Bijinesu no Atarashii Mantra
(Be-jee-nay-suu no Ah-tah-rah-she Mahn-toh-rah)

By the 1980s the overwhelming majority of the Japanese had begun subscribing to a concept that called for them to begin acting on the basis of principles rather than policies in order to put themselves in harmony with the rest of the world. The key word in this new concept was *kyosei* (k'yoe-say-e), meaning "symbiosis", or, in this case, mutually beneficial cooperative alliances with the rest of the world.

Businesspeople, politicians and others now routinely proclaim that *kyosei* between all of the economies of the world is the only way to achieve both economic prosperity and peace, and the concept has become their new business mantra.

This paradigm shift in Japan's economic policy offers foreign businesspeople new opportunities in Japan, as more and more Japanese companies seek joint ventures and other kinds of relationships with foreign firms.

Veteran Japanese-American management consultant Earle Okumura says the opportunities presented by Japan today should not be limited to Japan. He recommends that Western companies wanting to do business in China first establish an operation base in Japan, where the conditions are stable and predictable, and then go into China.

Obviously, the economies of the world are being integrated, but the motivation is profit-making rather than globalization for the sake of humanity. The Japanese concept of *kyosei* includes the concept of oneness for mutual benefit, and it should be promoted.

Companies in the U.S. and in Europe are gradually creating a new paradigm for corporate governance that is more human-centered. It would seem that the situation in Japan and in the world at large offers an opportunity for corporations East and West to use the Japanese concept of *kyosei* to fuse the best parts of their management practices and come up with a universal approach that would be much closer to meeting human needs.

12

The Forward Looking Attitude

Maemuki na Shisei
(My-muu-kee nah She-say-ee)

One of the most important factors in the economic success of Japan was a total reversal of the traditional samurai concept of revering the past and maintaining the status quo—a system that had bound them in a time warp for nearly a thousand years. When the last pillars of this system were eliminated in 1945/6, the Japanese were brimming with more than a thousand years' worth of suppressed ambition and energy.

Eventually, this new concept and spirit was expressed in the term *maemuki na shisei* (my-muu-kee nah she-say-ee), which translates as "forward looking attitude," and now incorporates the concept of planning and preparing for a high-tech future that is virtually unlimited.

What is especially significant is that this effort is being coordinated on a national level by a number of government ministries, major corporate conglomerates and universities—a factor that gives the Japanese an advantage over the United States and European countries where competing interests and different values prevent such mass cooperation.

Maemuki na shisei, organized on a national scale, is a cultural force that could and should be emulated by the West.

13

Pride as an Economic Force

Hokorubeki Keizai Ryoku
(Hoh-koh-rue-bay-kee Kay-ee-zigh R'yoh-kuu)

Pride has been one of the most important elements in Japan's history. Pride in race, pride in culture, and pride in country have been major ingredients in the character of the Japanese since ancient times, and has provided them with much of the energy and motivation that has made them so powerful and so successful in many ways.

It is surely accurate to say that without the extraordinary pride that has been a hallmark of the Japanese character throughout their history, Japan would still be a third world country.

But as in so many other facets of the Japanese character it was the samurai who took the pride of the Japanese to sublime heights. The samurai code required a level of self-image, self-confidence, and honor on such a high plane that their pride took precedence over the value of their lives as well as the lives of others.

It was the pride and passion of the samurai that helped make it possible for them to go from an agrarian and handicraft economy to a modern industrialized nation in twenty years. It was the legacy of this samurai pride that helped make it possible for them to come back after the debacle of World War II and build the world's second largest economy in less than thirty years.

This same pride is still today what makes the Japanese such formidable people. There is no area of Japanese life that is not influence by this pride. The quality of the products they make, the way they dress, the way they work, the amazing efficiency of their transportation systems, all of these things and more are manifestations of the pride the Japanese have as a people and as a country.

There are other cultures in the world that produce men with great pride, but in many countries this pride is used to abuse and repress others rather than to uplift society. The world needs a mandatory primer on the nature and role of a universal, human-oriented pride—something that surely would reduce the amount of violence in the world as well as promote the inevitable globalism.

14

Nationalism as an Economic Force

Keizai Ryoku to Minzokushugi
(Kay-ee-zigh R'yoh-kuu toh Meen-zoh-kuu-shuu-ghee)

Shortly after Emperor Hirohito announced Japan's surrender to the Allied Forces in mid-August 1945, dozens of people gathered on the grounds in front of the Imperial Palace and committed suicide.

In November 1970, Yukio Mishima, one of Japan's most brilliant novelists and playwrights who was also a Rightist with his own private army, forced his way into the headquarters of Japan's National Defense Force in central Tokyo, went out on a balcony, and in a long speech beseeched the soldiers who had gathered around the building to reject all things modern and go back to the old ways.

Mishima then committed *harakiri* in the way of the samurai, by plunging a short dagger into the left side of his stomach and stretching his neck out to make it easier for his *kaishakunin* (kigh-shah-kuu-neen), or aide, to cut his head off.

Unfortunately, Mishima had selected a famous old sword for his *kaishakunin* to use to decapitate him after he made the first cut in his stomach. The sword must have been quite dull or the *kaishakunin* a very inexperienced swordsman because it took him three strokes to completely severe Mishima's head.*

There have been no reported incidents of formal *harakiri* in Japan since Mishima dispatched himself in 1970. But it is still fairly common for business people and others to commit suicide to take responsibility for grievous mistakes. The dedication and sacrificial spirit symbolized by *harakiri* continues to play a significant role in present-day Japan, encouraging students to study and workers to sacrifice themselves, and often their families, to the survival and growth of their companies.

Mishima's call for political nationalism and a return to the past was a total failure. The samurai spirit of old had already been transformed into economic ambitions and nationalism, and was the source of the extraordinary energy and diligence that made it possible for Japan to become an economic superpower.

It is still common today for businesspeople, bureaucrats and politicians alike to invoke the spirit of the stomach-cutting samurai in their efforts to serve the economic interests of Japan.

Love of one's own country is, of course, a common human attribute. The problem is this love is often expressed in narrow minded, negative destructive ways. Until it becomes world-based instead of country-based, friction and conflicts will continue.

Committing suicide in Japan today can be very expensive. When the act results in the stoppage of a train, for example, the individual's family may receive a bill for several million yen for the inconvenience and cost involved.

---

* I met Mishima in the 1960s in the lobby of the Imperial Hotel for a discussion that lasted for about an hour. He gave no inkling, and I had no prescience, of his ultimate end.

15
The Power of Dignity

Hinkaku no Chikara
(Heen-kah-kuu no Chee-kah-rah)

One of the distinguishing characteristics of Japan's samurai class was a level of dignity, expressed both verbally and physically, that we in the West normally associate with kings and queens and other members of royal courts.

As a result of the pervasive influence of this highly dignified samurai culture, the Japanese have been conditioned for centuries to be especially sensitive to *hinkaku* (heen-kah-kuu), or "dignified behavior", and to expect people in responsible positions to be paragons of *hinkaku*. The higher and more important a person's position, the more the Japanese expect that person to exemplify dignity.

A significant reason why the early Japanese tended to look down on the first Westerners to visit Japan was that they did not demonstrate the qualities of *hinkaku* that the Japanese had come to expect of everyone [not to mention the fact that the Westerners didn't bathe, stank to high heaven, and routinely broke virtually every etiquette rule that made up the Japanese Way].

Still today, the foreign businessman or politician who fails to behave at an acceptable level of *hinkaku* suffers a serious loss of face, which reinforcing the general Japanese belief that theirs is a superior culture. Traditionally, the only socially accepted occasion when people could drop their mask of dignity was when they were in the institutionalized setting of drinking parties at geisha houses, bars, cabarets and other private places where drinking takes place.

Foreigners who want to be accepted by the Japanese as sincere, virtuous, dependable, and worthy as friends and as allies or partners, are advised to make sure they exhibit an ample degree of *hinkaku* on all other occasions. In other words, dignity is associated with the highest cultural values.

The Chad Rowan/Akebono sumo story was a classic example of the role of dignity in present-day Japanese culture. Rowan, an American who became a sumo wrestler in the 1980s, advanced rapidly up the ranks of sumodom to *Ozeki* (Oh-zay-kee) or Champion, causing a great deal of concern among the lords of sumo because they were afraid that if they promoted him to *Yokozuna* (Yoh-koh-zuu-ba), or Grand Champion, he would disgrace the sport.

But Rowan-Akebono kept winning tournaments, and following his victory in the January 1993 sumo tournament the Sumo Association judges were so impressed with his behavior that they unanimously confirmed him as Japan's first foreign sumo Grand Champion—an event as auspicious as the marriage of Emperor Akihito, the then Crown Prince, to a commoner, Michiko Shoda, in 1959.

Japan's traditional samurai-inspired culture instilled a sense of dignity in everyone, down to common laborers. Refined manners were one of the primary imperatives of the samurai code of ethics, and the code was enforced to the point that it became an integral part of the culture, and was both absorbed naturally and taught rigorously to everyone.

The dignified behavior of the Japanese has served them admirably in their dealings with foreigners, especially Americans who tend to equate dignified manners with an upper class pedigree that includes a high level of education and morality.

The built-in *hinkaku* of the Japanese has thus served them as an important business asset, and is something that Westerners, again Americans in particular, should recognize as an important element in their relationships with Japanese, and, in this case, not be caught with their *hinkaku* pants down.

The level of dignified behavior in the Western world varies widely with class, education, ethnicity, geographical region, and so on. Among the major countries, it is probably lower in the United States than anywhere else. It goes without saying that life in the United States would be more peaceful, more genteel, and more satisfying if the level of dignity was raised through both example and education.

The ultimate demonstration of the dignity of the samurai was no doubt the performance of the ritual of *seppuku* (sape-puu-kuu) (harakiri). It was as precise, as refined and as dignified, as the tea ceremony.

16

The Power of Extreme Diligence

Osokubeki Nihonjin no Kinben
(Oh-soh-kuu-bay-kee Nee-hoan-jeen no Keen-bane)

One of the most powerful elements in the amazing success story of Japan is the extreme diligence that the vast majority of the people bring to whatever task is at hand. Their diligence has traditionally been driven by both unbounded pride in race and culture, and in an equally powerful urge to demonstrate their equality—if not their superiority—to other people. All of which are traits that were dramatically enhanced by the samurai and thereafter became deeply embedded in the common culture.

A story that I have told before reveals the fact that the concept of diligence and all that it implies is typically in the forefront of the Japanese consciousness. I was at a convention in New York, came down from my hotel room at 6 a.m. for breakfast and encountered a Japanese whom I had met several times in Tokyo, also waiting to be seated.

I said to him in Japanese; "Good morning! You're up early, aren't you!"

He replied forcefully with no hint of a smile: *Kinben-na Nihonjin desu kara!* (Because I am a diligent Japanese!)

It apparently did not impress him that I was up and that the dining room was already full of Americans who were up even earlier than either of us.

During the samurai era in Japan, diligence achieved virtual cult status. The fabled *Yamato Damashii* (Yah-mah-toh Dah-mah-she-ee), or "Spirit of Japan", which went back to the 8th century, equated diligence with being Japanese, and being able to accomplish any task.

During the early post-World War II years the term *kinbensei* (keen-bane-say-ee) or "spirit of diligence" became virtually synonymous with *Nihonjin* (Nee-hoan-jeen), the word for a Japanese person—and one constantly heard the terms used together in *kinben-na Nihonjin* (keen-bane-nah Nee-hohn-jeen), or "diligent Japanese."

During that time the Japanese automatically attributed much of their phenomenal success to being far more diligent than other people. By the 1980s, however, the situation had begun to change dramatically. Japan's postwar generations, especially those born after 1970, were no longer culturally imbued with compulsive *kinbensei*. Raised without knowing hunger or fear, and inundated with toys, clothing, entertainment devices, and other distractions, this generation grew up in a different world.

Younger Japanese are no longer blindly driven by a cultural superiority complex or by unbounded pride. Their loyalty and dedication to Japan are real enough, but they are no longer obsessive. This change in the character of younger Japanese is one of the most serious concerns facing the country today. In the government as well as in corporate Japan, older officials and executives are fighting a rear-guard battle to preserve as much of the cultural *kinbensei* of the Japanese as possible.*

The challenge they face may not be as serious as they believe, because they are comparing present-day Japanese with earlier generations, which took diligence to an extreme. Still today, typical Japanese employees are more diligent than most of their Western counterparts, and *kinbensei* remains an important economic asset.

Other cultures teach various levels of diligence, with Americans, British, French, Germans, Jews and others high on the list, but none surpass the Japanese. Furthermore, on an overall scale the built-in diligence of Westerners in advanced countries appears to have diminished in recent decades.

This is another area where taking a page from Bushido and adapting it to the Western environment, would provide a significant cultural boost across the board.

---

* In pre-World War II Japan, the diligence of Japanese students was incredible. It was common for youths studying Japanese-English dictionaries to memorize a page and then eat it to organically absorb it into the body.

17

The Power of Kata

Kata wo Anadorubekarazu
(Kah-tah no Ah-nah-doh-rue-bay-kah-rah-zuu)

In the book *KATA—The Key to Understanding & Dealing With the Japanese*, I proposed the theory that virtually every aspect of the typical, traditional Japanese mindset, their attitudes and their behavior, were the product of specific, precise *kata* (kah-tah), or ways of doing things, that had been ritualized and sanctified over the centuries, and went on to explain the origin of the kata and how they continued to influence the Japanese today.

The samurai class that began emerging in Japan in the 13th century adopted the same precise *kata*-ized patterns of physical and mental training that had originated in Shinto rituals and in the master-apprentice approach of the arts and crafts industries.

Some of Japan's traditional *kata*-based practices and skills that remain in place today include the tea ceremony, flower arranging, kendo, judo and sumo. Even the imported sport of baseball has been partially *kata*-ized.*[1] There is a Japanized way to arrange furniture and office desks, for learning how to drive, for treating guests, for buying and presenting gifts, for virtually everything in life.

Following the end of the Shogunate government in 1868, elementary and high school level education was meticulously structured with very specific *kata* that ranged from identical uniforms to strict routines for classroom and schoolyard behavior. The new Western style military organizations also adopted the *kata*-ized samurai way of training and disciplining troops.*² The system was designed to mold each student and soldier into a homogenized product of the samurai culture.

From then on until the early 1990s, companies and organizations of all types interviewing employee recruits simply weeded out candidates who did not fit the *kata*-ized national mold.

The subjection of all Japanese to this strict molding process during childhood and their teen years further strengthened the common set of "Japanese" characteristics that were to play a seminal role in the country's future—more so than in the past because this time the system was directly applied to everyone, not just the privileged samurai class. These characteristics included:

1) A compulsion to work together in clearly defined, exclusive groups.
2) Fierce loyalty to their groups and to Japan.

---

*¹ When first imported into Japan, baseball was totally *kata*-ized, with results that were shocking to the professional American players who began joining the Japanese clubs in the 1950s. This peculiar phenomenon was described by journalist-author Robert Whiting in a marvelous best selling book called *You Gotta Have Wa* (Macmillan) in the 1980s. *Wa* (wah) means "harmony."

*² An American military observer who witnessed the training of Japanese troops during the Russo-Japan war in 1904–05 questioned a commander about forcing his troops to march in frigid weather for three days and nights without allowing them to sleep. The commander's response: "They know how to sleep. They need training in how to stay awake!"

3) A highly developed sense of balance, form, order and style.

4) An intuitive feel (and need) for precision, accuracy and correctness.

5) Extraordinary manual dexterity and the ability to work especially well on small, sophisticated objects.

6) A predisposition to apply themselves with single-minded dedication to the task at hand.

7) An overwhelming desire to excel in anything they did; to be as good as or better than anyone else—although if they were better than members of their own group they had to downplay their talent behind a mask of humility in order to maintain internal harmony.

As can readily be appreciated, an entire nation physically and mentally conditioned in these attributes is going to have a significant advantage over people who are less trained, especially when their efforts are channeled by the government and industry to achieve specific goals.

I have long said that the Japanese have too many *kata* and Americans have too few. Little by little, the Japanese are losing their *kata*-ized culture. The weaker the *kata* become and the more of them that disappear, the weaker the Japanese will be in everything that they do.

American culture, as mixed as it is, would be greatly enhanced by the creation and application of *kata*-ized learning procedures that go well beyond the present system.

This should begin at a very young age with such simple things as table manners, keeping one's clothing and possessions in a neat and orderly way, using polite language to others, penmanship, reading and composing poetry, learning such manual skills as craft-making, and making simple repairs of one kind or another.

18

The Perfectionism Factor

Kanzenshugi no Yohso
(Kahn-zen-shuu-ghee no Yohh-soh)

Japan's traditional culture contained the premise that artists and craftsmen should strive for perfection throughout their lives; that there was no end to such efforts. The samurai adopted this theme and took it even further, making it a virtual obsession. Over the centuries, this philosophy permeated the whole of Japanese culture, and still today continues to play a vital role in the lives of the Japanese.

There are numerous historical and contemporary examples of the power of this factor in Japanese culture, some mundane and others on a metaphysical plane.

There was a scene in the epic *Shogun* that was a wonderful metaphor for all of the metaphysical facets and goals of Japan's traditional culture. It was the scene in which the foreign protagonist, played by Richard Chamberlain, challenged a samurai by boasting that as a weapon his pistol was superior to the samurai's bow—and implied that he represented a more advanced and powerful culture.

Chamberlain demonstrated his prowess with the pistol, and then waited for the samurai to take his turn. The samurai chose as his target one of the wooden gateposts in front of the house they were in. While still seated on the tatami reed-mat floor, the samurai, moving with controlled efficiency and speed, notched an arrow and let it fly through the closed paper door that totally blocked his view of the target.

The samurai could not see his target. Ostensibly, he did not aim. And although the film did not literally show that his arrow had indeed pierced its target, it was clearly understood that it had done so. And such was the psychic force of the experience that the astounded foreigner did not question the assumption that the samurai's arrow had found its mark.

Defying Common Sense

What the samurai had done was demonstrate that the mastery of any art or skill has two dimensions—the physical and the mental, and that the mental aspect may defy the rules of Western style logic and common sense.

This aspect of Japan's traditional culture is, in fact, repeatedly portrayed in the country's famed *chambara* (chaam-bah-rah) historical period films that depict the skills—albeit often times exaggerated—of the samurai of old. Those who took their training seriously, or were naturally gifted, developed a "sixth sense" that made it possible for them to feel and "see" things that were not visible to the naked eye—and therefore to accomplish what appeared to be incredible feats.

It was this metaphysical ability that marked the difference between the ordinary and the great; between the master and the highly trained and experienced but still run-of-the-mill bowman, swordsman, painter, potter or garden designer.

Achieving a State of Muga

Historically, training in Japan combined the mental and the mechanical, with mind-training often taking precedence over the physical. The ultimate goal of the training was to achieve a perfect meld between the body and the mind, resulting in a state described as *muga* (muu-gah)—meaning, in simple terms, that the body and the mind functioned as one: that there were no hang-ups, no barriers between thinking and doing. So powerful was this *muga*-mind state that spirit frequently transcended matter.

In part, at least, it was this background of spiritual as well as physical training that made the Japanese a formidable people in whatever they set out to do. And although the philosophy and discipline that characterized the cultural conditioning of the Japanese during their long feudal age (1192–1945) has changed dramatically since the 1950s, the influence of this heritage continues to play a significant role in many key areas of Japanese life.

In more modern terms, Japan's contemporary version of *muga* manifests itself in the extraordinary degree of concentration, dedication and diligence that they focus on goals. The aim in every endeavor is to get as close as possible to perfection, then continue pushing the envelope.

Present-day Japan's most devoted cadre of businessmen and higher ranking government officials are the philosophical and spiritual descendants of the master warriors of the past, and bring many of their *muga*-like attitudes to the table.

The Role of Zen

Much of the theory and techniques behind the power and practice of *muga*-enhanced attitudes and behavior comes from Zen: that branch of Buddhism that has the most to do with the visible world, even though it teaches that what we perceive as real exists only in our minds. At the same time, however, Zen also teaches that to be in harmony with the tangible world at large, and to control it to our advantage, the first and last requirement is control of the mind.

Extrapolating on this concept, the only way anyone can master anything to the point of perfection is through Zen—or its equivalent in whatever culture is concerned. The Zen way to *muga* incorporates focusing and thinking positively to the exclusion of everything else, along with using the power of the mind and imagination to "create" the desired result—all of which are common sense concepts, and yet, use of this knowledge around the world, particularly in the West, is rare.

In the West, oddly enough, about the only area of human endeavor that has generally accepted the validity and merit of the *muga* mind, and attempted to institutionalize it, is professional sports, especially in golf (where the slightest deviation between the mind and the body is the difference between being successful and unsuccessful).

However, virtually all successful men and women have used *muga* in their efforts, regardless of whether they did so consciously, or what they might have considered the secrets of their success.

I believe I have had one true *muga*-based experience, and it was one of the most unreal and exhilarating events of my life. The occasion was a Sunday morning bowling session at the Tokyo Bowling Center years ago. When I picked up the ball and made my approach to the alley, it was as if I were in a dream, observing myself, and not directly or consciously controlling my body. I knew I was going to roll a strike. It was as if I had already done so and my body was just acting out the confirmation. The same thing happened on my second effort, and again on my third. But when I got up to bowl the fourth time, the *muga* union between my mind and body suddenly evaporated. There was no unity, no effortless focus. The results were a foregone conclusion.

For most of us, the experience of seeing things go awry because we cannot control our minds or our bodies is the common one. Hopefully, the day will soon arrive when the *muga* concept will become an integral part of all of our education and training.

The Perfectionists

Japan's traditional culture therefore tended to produce people who were *korisho* (koe-ree-show), or "perfection-oriented"—another key Japanese term I introduced in *Japan's Cultural Code Words: 233 Key Terms That Explain Japanese Attitudes and Behavior*. Anything less than perfect immediately caught their eye. Even if an imperfection was so slight it was barely noticeable, it would be conspicuous to the Japanese and they would reject the product.

Although the Japanese penchant for perfection has weakened considerably in recent decades, it is still a significant factor in their reaction to everything—from how one holds and uses chopsticks to the stitching on a label inside a piece of clothing.

Westerners wanting to do business in Japan can take it for granted that they will encounter the *korisho* factor, and should take steps to deal with it before showing their products—a process that often includes giving the product a "Japanese touch."

Understanding the Japanese compulsion for form, order, quality, and their aesthetic tastes is essential before the foreign business can establish a basis for communicating with its Japanese counterparts. Prospective deals with Japanese companies can evaporate if the foreign side presents an unstructured, disordered image, even if its products meet the Japanese test.

Obviously, people interested in doing business in Japan must also be prepared to raise certain product standards to meet those of the Japanese, rather than expect the Japanese to lower their standards.

"The Japanese did not invent the light bulb or put a man on the moon. But if it weren't for their discipline and perfectionism, we wouldn't be challenged to continuously improve the quality of everything we do."—*Joe Schmelzeis.*

Form as Realty

The Japanese concept of *shi kata* (she kah-tah), or "way of doing things," includes more than just the mechanical process of doing something. It also incorporates the physical and spiritual laws of the cosmos. It refers to the way things are supposed to be done, both the form and the order, as a means of expressing and maintaining *wa* (wah), "harmony," in society and the universe. The absence of *shikata* is virtually unthinkable to the Japanese, for that refers to an unreal world, without order or form.

Early in their history the Japanese developed the belief that form had a reality of its own, and that it often took precedence over substance. They also believed that anything could be accomplished if the right process was mentally and physically practiced long enough.

Just as there was only one acceptable way to perform all the various actions of life in pre-industrial Japan, from using chopsticks to wrapping a package, there was naturally only one right way of thinking—the "Japanese" way. Cultural conditioning based on the *kata* system made the Japanese extremely sensitive to any thought, manner, or action that did not conform perfectly to the appropriate *kata*.

This is another cultural dimension that the Japanese tended to take too far in human terms, but it nevertheless was a major factor in their rise to economic prominence. Taught in a more flexible way, *korisho* could contribute significantly to the quality of products and the ambience of life, and is therefore something else the West could learn from the samurai.

19

Tapping into Cosmic Wisdom

Uchuu no Chie to Dohka suru Chikara
(Uu-chuu no Chee-eh toh Doh-kh sue-rue Chee-kah-rah)

One of the aspects of Zen that has played a significant role in Japan for centuries is what might be called cosmic wisdom—something that until recently the Western world tended to regard as mystic nonsense (unless it was a Christian religious dogma).

In fact, it was not until the latter part of the 20th century that Western scientists began to accept the idea that their concepts of the physical world were only a part of the human as well as the cosmic equation. More and more Westerners now recognize that there is more to life and the cosmos than meets the unaided eye.

Asians, on the other hand, have been tapping into cosmic wisdom for several thousand years—a phenomenon that was to reach new and very practical heights with Japan's Zen-made samurai.

As noted in another of my books (*The Japanese Have a Word*

for It), Zen advocates learned a long time ago that conventional wisdom and judgment always obscure reality, and that until one is able to rid oneself of programmed perceptions, one cannot see reality, achieve personal freedom, or transcend the perceived limitations of the physical world.

Zen practitioners also learned that physical skills could be developed to an astounding degree through a systematic program of Zen techniques—and this was one of the primary reasons why Japan's famed samurai adopted Zen Buddhism as an essential part of their training in the use of the sword and other weapons.

The aim of the samurai was to meld the mind and the body in such a way that they could virtually transform thought into reality—achieving remarkable physical and mental feats, one of which was the ritual of *seppuku* or *harakiri* as it is better known in the West—a method of self-destruction that took incredible will.

Cosmic-Powered Thought

Zen continues to play a significant role in Japan today, in business, in the arts and crafts, in design and other intellectual pursuits, including the writing of poetry. One of the modern versions of Zen in today's business world is known as *jizai* (jee-zigh), which may be translated as "personal freedom."

Jizai refers to being able to think freely without being influenced by custom, conventional wisdom or any other preconceptions. It became very conspicuous in the 1950s when thousands of new companies sprang up in post-war Japan and began designing and producing products that broke all of the old traditions.

Virtually all of Japan's best-known businessmen-innovators now practice *jizai* in one form or another, and it is the underlying philosophy of think-tanks, the best-known of which is probably the *Jizai Kenkyu Jo* (Jee-zigh Kane-que Joh), or "Jizai Research

Institute", founded in 1970 by Masahiro Mori, a Tokyo University professor of engineering who was also a founder of the Robotics Society of Japan.

Many of the most impressive products developed in Japan since the 1970s have come out of *jizai* creative sessions, and the use of "personal freedom" in coming up with new concepts and products is increasing. In simple terms, *jizai*-thinking involves meditating until one achieves the ultimate truth or reality of a thing or idea. In product terms, this means the ultimate in function, refined simplicity and beauty.

The *jizai* approach to creativity has been described as refining and recycling, as in reincarnation. Each time the product is recycled it is improved.

Much of the creative activity in Japanese companies is done by *go-nin gumi* (go-neen guu-me), or "five-person groups," an institutionalized team-size that goes back some 2,000 years in Japan's history because it was found to be an optimum number for getting the most out of group responsibility and effort. [Numerous organizational studies in Japan have also shown that the maximum number of sections, departments or divisions that an individual manager can handle effectively is five.]

Westerners might be much more comfortable with the idea of using cosmic wisdom in their work and personal affairs if it was expressed in terms of intuition or common sense—both or which generally require a period of thought (meditation!) before they can be successfully engaged.

The deliberate practice of *jizai* as one of the first steps in the creative process would certainly be an easy custom to adopt.

20

Using the Power of Ki

Ki no Chikara wo Tsukau
(Kee no Chee-kah-rah oh T'sue-kow)

There is growing evidence that ancient Asians discovered some of the fundamental secrets of the universe through introspection rather than scientific research. The existence and power of *ki* (kee) is one of these secrets, and is something that a number of Japanese businessmen are applying in their personal and employee training programs.

I have seen martial arts demonstrations in which an elderly master—a slender wisp of a man who could weigh no more than sixty kilograms—ostensibly made not one but several husky young men go flying though the air at the same time without appearing to exert any effort at all—by simply touching the one who was in front of the line-up attacking him.

These demonstrations were held to show the power of *ki* (kee)—something that few Westerners had ever heard of until the term appeared in the mid–1990s in a number of mass-circulated

American news magazines.*

The concept, and use, of *ki* is ancient in Asia. Several thousand years ago in India and China, men learned through introspection that the blood circulates through the body (something that was discovered in Europe only a few hundred years ago), and that there is some kind of "life force" that permeates the body, can be manipulated by the mind, and reacts to the touch and to the insertion of needles into the pathways of this energy.

This early knowledge and use of a special mind-body power was not exclusive to Asia, however. It seems that most, if not all, ancient cultures in the West and throughout the world were aware of and made use of cosmic energy in some of their activities. But in Western Europe, in particular, Christianity linked such practices with the Devil, and later empirical scientists disavowed anything they could not see or prove in their laboratories.

It was not until the last decades of the 20th century that some Americans and Europeans, influenced by increasing contacts with Japan, China and other Asian countries, began to relearn the old knowledge that the body is infused with a kind of energy and that this energy can be focused by the mind to alter blood pressure, control pain and do other physical things that Western scientists and medical authorities had long regarded as absolute nonsense.

A primary stimulus for this interest among Westerners was the practice of acupuncture, and its growing popularity among certain doctors. This interest was greatly fanned when high profile American journalist Scotty Reston suffered a sudden appendicitis attack when he was in Beijing, was operated on by Chinese surgeons who used only acupuncture as an anesthesia, and later published a glowing account of his experience in *The New York Times*.

---

* It was introduced much earlier in a number of my books on Japan, including *Japan's Cultural Code Words* (Tuttle Publishing Company).

Researching the Mysterious Energy

In the 1980s, the Chinese government launched a major research program, using modern scientific methods, to prove not only the existence of this extraordinary "life force" in people, but also its efficacy in treating a variety of ailments. The government also sponsored the establishment of dozens of regional schools to annually train thousands of individuals in the use of acupuncture.

Ki is variously translated as "energy", "spirit", "mind" and "cosmic breath". It is one of the syllables in *aikido* (aye-kee-doh), one of Japan's popular martial arts. It is also a key part of the term *kiai* (kee-aye), which is the shout or cry that kendo practitioners utter when attacking an opponent with their bamboo swords.

The Japanese and other Asians learned long ago that one can marshal or summon up the power of *ki* for a sudden burst of energy by shouting. This shout does not have to be *kiai* itself. It can be any sound, with or without a meaning.

In the 1960s, many Japanese corporations began programs to strengthen the *ki* of new employees and to teach them how to use it in their business activities. Newly hired recruits were sent to military-type training centers where they were required to spend an hour or more each day shouting as loud as they could in some public place; often in front of local train stations where commuters were constantly coming and going.

Regardless of how such practices might sound to the rational and scientific-minded Western businessperson, they work—as anyone who has served in a marine-type military unit or engaged in certain sports activities can testify. Although diminished somewhat, it is common to see company employees in front of train stations, yelling out messages of one kind or another, more to build their self-confidence and aggressiveness than to sell products.

I will not make any predictions about Western companies adopting *kiai* training for their employees, or suggest that they should, but with some new twists the concept of *ki*, and some of its more astounding uses, are on their way to becoming accepted universally.

Since the mid–1980s a growing number of Japan's best-known and most influential businessmen have been flocking to *ki* masters to learn how to make "the force" work for them. In the 1990s, Japan's powerful and prestigious Ministry of International Trade and Industry began working with the University of Electro-Communications to try to find out what *ki* is and how to harness it. Sony Corporation, the epitome of a modern, international company, also has a scientific team studying the phenomenon of *ki*.

According to the testimony of several top-level executives in some of Japan's largest and most successful companies, including Sony and Sega Enterprises, *ki* has cured ailments, made them more youthful and energetic, and given them extraordinary insight into managing their companies. With this kind of endorsement, and given the follow-the-successful-company syndrome that is characteristic of the Japanese, *ki* may very well play an increasingly important role in Japan's economic arsenal.

It may therefore behoove Western businesspeople as well to seriously look into the potential of *ki*, not only to maintain their competitive edge but for the personal benefits that go with it. If the Chinese and Japanese efforts to understand and harness *ki* are successful, the rest of the world's businesspeople had better not be caught [this time!] with their *ki* pants down.

21

The
"Peace of Mind" Culture

Kokoro no Yasuragi no Bunka
(Koh-koh-roh no Yah-sue-rah-ghee no Boon-kah)

The foundation for all business relationships in Japan is the kind and degree of trust that creates "peace of mind," or *anshinkan* (ahn-sheen-kahn), one of the most powerful phrases in Japanese culture, and a major factor in the samurai code of ethics. In fact, Bushido required the samurai to take extreme measures to achieve peace of mind, and to expect it in others as well.

Newcomers or outsiders can establish an *anshinkan* relationship with a Japanese enterprise by going through a kind of ritualized period of getting acquainted and establishing bonds based on the good character and personal responsibility of the individuals involved.

This process may be complicated because the Japanese have difficulty accepting and working with individuals who are not members of recognized or readily identifiable organizations; and they have the same problem working with companies they do not know. This makes it necessary for the lone entrepreneur and the representative of an unknown company to provide sufficient proof that they are trustworthy, and can be relied upon to do all of the things that are necessary to avoid failure and not embarrass anyone.

One of the ways for the entrepreneur and newcomer to penetrate this "peace" barrier is to first develop a network of contacts in banks and other businesses to give themselves substance, because in the beginning newcomers are like the invisible man; people look right through them. Major foreign firms coming into Japan naturally have an advantage, but their representatives must go through a similar qualifying process. The success of their companies at home is not automatically accepted as evidence that they can be trusted and will not fail in Japan.

Building Peace of Mind

Still today, the desire for *anshinkan* in Japan has a direct impact on all areas of public life, and in particular on business relations. Businesspeople prefer not to do business with others until they know them well and have confidence in their ability, honesty, goodwill, and dependability, and feel "peace of mind" in dealing with them.

In fact, there have probably been as many failures in Japan by famous and successful foreign companies as by medium-sized and smaller firms, mostly because the larger firms did not do the things that are essential for building trust and peace of mind.

Naturally foreign businesspeople wanting to do business in Japan should naturally be aware of the role of *anshinkan*, and make it a significant part of their approach and ongoing relations with Japanese companies. It also helps for the foreign side to publicly state to its Japanese counterparts that they desire a relationship based on *anshinkan*, and that all of its efforts will be designed to achieve that goal.

Among other things, the Japanese will be surprised that foreigners know the term, and the Japanese will be even more gratified to learn that foreigners view it as a desirable part of any relationship that develops.

Harmony/Spirit/Love/Sharing

Another of the samurai-promoted concepts that gradually seeped into the common cultural of Japan is expressed in the compound *wakiaiai* (wah-kee-aye-aye), which literally means "harmony/spirit/love/sharing," and refers to respect for and worship of the beauty of harmony in nature.

Wakiaiai is one of Japan's many cultural code words that originally referred to the idealized harmonious relationship between people, and came to be associated with the feeling that harmony should be the overriding principle in business relationships as well—especially between managers and their employees.

Westerners typically have difficulty interacting efficiently with Japanese because the *wakiaiai* factor requires that the Japanese give precedence to time-consuming consensus and group harmony, the latter oftentimes on a level that never seems to end.

Because this kind of harmony has been a fundamental ethic in Japanese society for many centuries, it is not going to disappear any time soon. Westerners doing business in Japan will simply have to accommodate themselves to a different way of thinking and doing things.

Better yet, they might find it to their advantage to adopt the *wakiaiai* principle in developing and nurturing their relationships with the Japanese, and with others as well.

Magic Words in Business Harmony

Bijinesu de Seiko suru tame no Magikku Waado
(Bee-jee-nay-sue day Say-ee-koh sue-rue tah-may no
Mah-jeek-kuu Waah-doh)

With the partial exception of the younger generations and a small percentage of mavericks, the daily behavior of the Japanese generally follows the rules and forms set down hundreds of years ago and enforced by the samurai code of ethics, particularly in business and formal situations. Age, sex, rank and relationship continue to be of vital importance in determining appropriate behavior between individuals.

The ideal for all interpersonal relationships in Japanese society is described by the term *enman* (inn-mahn), which means "perfection", "harmony", "smoothness" and "peace"—a concept that applies more precisely to human behavior than the more popular word *wa* (wah), or "harmony."

One of the methods used by the Japanese to smooth the way in business, political and personal relationships and achieve *enman* is subsumed in the common idiomatic expression *suriawase* (sue-ree-ah-wah-say), which may be translated as "adjustment of views." [*Suri* appears in compounds referring to rubbing things together until they are smooth; grinding away the roughness.]

The use of *suriawase* in all relationships in Japan prevents either side from regarding itself as a winner or a loser, while protecting both sides from loss of face or injured feelings.

Suriawase is used in all business relationships, starting out with the initial negotiations and continuing on through the life of the relationship. It is, in fact, the ongoing process that the Japanese use to keep their business relationships moving along as smoothly as possible.

As mentioned earlier, the Japanese make a major point of emphasizing that circumstances change constantly, and that for two companies to work together in a mutually acceptable manner it is essential that their views, and often their operating procedures, be adjusted accordingly on a regular basis.

This is one of the reasons why the Japanese have always felt uncomfortable with very precise and very tight contracts that do not allow flexibility in a relationship, and why there is frequent friction with their foreign partners when they assume the right to "adjust" the terms of such contracts.

Anyone who has ever been involved in negotiating sessions with Japanese businesspeople and politicians can fully appreciate the concept of "grinding" away all the differences in viewpoints, goals, and expectations. Negotiating sessions may go on for days, weeks, and months, and often times the ultimate "winner" is the side that was able to sit the longest, slowly grinding away at the other party's resolve.

As has been noted before, the Western approach to maintaining good relations and in negotiating is based on choosing among different options. The Japanese approach is based on compromising on points, leaving the final decision or agreement flexible, and allowing for minor infringements that do not disturb the relationship.

This is what the Japanese call the *awase* (ah-wah-say) approach, and it applies to both conversations and business deals. The basic meaning of *awase* is "to unite, to join things together." In practical use it means "You adjust to my position, and I will adjust to yours."

Because of the uncertainty that this approach suggests, Westerners often find it difficult to deal with, and may regard it as insincere or dishonest. It is neither. It is the Japanese way of dealing with unknowns and variables, which is an advantage if both parties are playing by the same rules and communicate regularly.

One of the ways the Japanese use to reduce the amount of time spent at *suriawase* is to engage in separate sessions of *nemawashi* (nay-mah-wah-she), especially after-hours during long eating and drinking bouts in restaurants, lounges, or cabarets.

Nemawashi originally referred to preparing a plant for transplanting. *Ne* means "root", and *mawashi* means "spin" or "turn." When used in the social sense, *nemawashi* refers to a combination of bargaining and subtle arm-twisting to win advocates for a cause, that is, turning roots around so they will "grow" the way you want.

When *suriawase* sessions take place in Japan, the Japanese have an obvious advantage because they are on their home ground. When the first meetings are to take place in Japan, the foreign side should set a reasonable time frame for completion of the talks, and make prearrangements so that if additional meetings are necessary, they will take place at their offices.

From the viewpoint of foreign businesspeople it is better to have the final rather than the first meetings on their own home ground, in order not to be put in a position of feeling under pressure because of time constraints, or because of the expense involved in staying in Japan, or for other reasons.

Another Magic Word

Tsukiai (t'sue-kee-aye) is another magic word in Japan. It is sometimes translated as "to associate with for the sake of friendship," but it goes well beyond the casual meaning this suggests, and is more like "social debt" or "social obligation." You "build" *tsukiai* with someone by associating with them, by helping them directly, and by doing favors for their families or close friends. They, in turn, can impose on the relationship when they want your cooperation or help.

Tsukiai is the oil that fuels business relationships in Japan. Businesspeople and professionals go out of their way to create "debt" relationships with people within their own organizations and in other companies and government offices for the day they will need some kind of help, service or cooperation.

Housewives work to build up a bank of *tsukiai* with teachers, doctors, and others whose goodwill and help they routinely need, primarily through gift-giving. On the business front, the most common way of building *tsukiai* relationships has traditionally been after-hours drinking and dining in bars, cabarets, and geisha houses. In the 1970s, golfing with business associates was added to this list.*

It is virtually impossible to do business with the Japanese without engaging in *tsukiai* activities because *tsukiai* remains an essential part of getting acquainted and building the personal trust that is the foundation for business relationships in Japan. The ability of

---

* One of the traditional methods of creating a *tsukiai* relationship between two men was for them to go an assignation house and have the same woman.

businesspeople to function effectively in Japan can be virtually ruined if they become known as *tsukiai ga warui hito* (t'sue-kee-aye gah wah-rue-ee ssh-toe), or "a person who is not good at making and nurturing social relationships."

Fortunately for foreign businessmen, and younger Japanese as well, who do not relish spending two, three, or more nights a week out drinking for the purpose of *tsukiai*, it is now generally possible to achieve the same ends through breakfast and lunch meetings, or through golf or some other sports activity once or twice a month, with evening affairs limited to every other month or so.

During vital negotiations, however, it is often necessary to have after-hours drinking sessions two or three times a week in order to keep the negotiation process going forward, because it is often only during such gatherings that the Japanese are able to speak frankly and clearly.

"Round of Greetings"

Another essential part of Japan's business and social etiquette that is very important for foreign businesspeople to understand and use to their own advantage is referred to in Japanese as *aisatsu* (aye-sot-sue), which is translated as "round of greetings", but has far deeper cultural nuances and uses than the English term suggests.

Aisatsu incorporates serious business as well as social obligations that must be fulfilled at the right time and in the right way to maintain favorable, effective relationships with all of the individuals who are important in one's life, from suppliers and customers to doctors, teachers, and favorite uncles.

The proper fulfillment of *aisatsu* obligations requires that on special occasions one make personal visits to the individuals involved to express appreciation, congratulations or condolences, depending on the circumstances, and that these visits conform to very traditional and ritualized forms.

These occasions include serious illnesses or accidents, funerals, weddings, the opening of new businesses, when new business relationships are established, and the like. The most important annual occasion calling for business *aisatsu* is the first official work day after New Year, usually between the 4th and 7th of January, depending on the company.

At this time, salesmen visit their customers; managers and executives visit their vendors, suppliers and bankers to acknowledge their business and support during the previous year and ask them to continue their patronage during the coming year. On a higher managerial level people engaging in *aisatsu* make appointments to ensure that the people they want to see will be available at the specified time.

In the typical company, very little work is done on *aisatsu* days, as the employees themselves celebrate the beginning of the New Year, and *aisatsu* visitors are coming and going. Many *aisatsu* visits include exchanging toasts with beer or *sake*, so it is common to see a lot of flushed faces on these days.

There are ritualized expressions that are used in *aisatsu* visits, and it behooves foreigners to learn some of these expressions. The most common is:

Saku nen chu wa taihen O'sewa ni narimashita. Mata kon nen mo yoroshiku O'negai itashimasu (Sah-kuu nane chuu wah tie-hane Oh-say-wah nee nah-ree-maash-tah. Mah-tah kone nane moh yoh-roh-she-kuu Oh-nay-guy-ee-tah-she-mah-suu).

A rather flowery translation of this phrase: "We are deeply obligated to you for your patronage and help last year, and extend our deepest gratitude. We ask that you please continue doing business with us this year."

Aisatsu visits are not empty formalities. They are key ingredients in the conduct of human relations in Japan. People take note and remember who follows the custom and who doesn't. Foreign businesspeople in Japan who are not aware of the tradition or who fail to give it its proper due are regarded as insensitive to the cultural mores of the country, and insincere in their personal behavior.

It is also important to remember that one does not discuss business during *aisatsu* meetings. Everyone already knows precisely why the visitors are calling on them.

Foreigners dealing with Japanese in country or abroad can significantly improve the quality of their relationships and help ensure that the relationship continues by following the *aisatsu* custom.

On a personal and social level *aisatsu* visits include gifts, which frequently consists of money. These visits may occur anytime during the year, and there are two institutionalized periods when gift-giving is a major national undertaking—*chugen* (chuu-gane) in August, and *O'seibo* (Oh-say-ee-boh) just before the end of the year. On these two occasions, individuals generally deliver gifts personally; companies have them delivered by parcel delivery firms.

Keeping Secrets

Unlike Americans and other Westerners who are prone to brag about their special skills, and to demonstrate them at every opportunity, the Japanese have been conditioned by their culture to develop one or more personal skills but to keep quiet about them, and then display them without any fanfare at an especially propitious moment.

These skills may be singing, a martial art, or some highly valued technology [and it occurs to me that the cultural reason for keeping them under wraps goes back to the days of the *Ninja*, the super spies, saboteurs and sometimes assassins of the samurai era.

These highly trained individuals had to be extremely careful not to display any of their talents in public because doing so would reveal their secret identity and alert their opponents].

The important point is that the Japanese have been culturally conditioned for centuries to develop a special *ude* (uu-day), literally "forearm", but the word is used colloquially to mean "ability" or "skill" in one or more areas, a factor that has contributed enormously to the economic achievements of the Japanese.

In keeping with their cultural traditions of humility and maintaining a low profile, the Japanese by their very nature do not brag about their *ude*, and are very careful about when and how they demonstrate it, in order to avoid appearing arrogant.

Not surprisingly, the Western custom of emphasizing one's schooling, experience, and expertise is one of the things that grates on the sensibilities of Japanese who associate with Westerners. Rather than brag about their accomplishments, the Japanese do not mention them at all, or they play them down—which is one of the reasons why Westerners so often underestimate them.

There are times, however, when it is appropriate for the Japanese to demonstrate their *ude*, and just one of these instances is after-hours in karaoke bars. These occasions are formally recognized as *ude no mise dokoro* (uu-day no me-say doh-koh-roh) or "the time and place to show one's ability."

Besides karaoke bars, other *ude no mise dokoro* include singing at company parties, putting on entertaining skits during company trips to resorts, participating in sports events, giving a humorous speech at weddings, and acting as the master of ceremonies at a company or social function.

In addition to these more social occasions, it is also appropriate for some people to demonstrate their technical or professional *ude* by presenting papers at conferences or playing a role in negotiating sessions. Demonstrating *ude* in negotiating sessions has to be carefully timed and coordinated, however, in order not to reveal one's skill or expertise too soon and thereby put the other side on guard.

Generally, the real experts in negotiations do not expound on the subject at hand—as Americans are wont to do. The experts may sit and say nothing, taking in everything the other side has to say, or they may ask question after question. It is often not until after formal negotiating sessions, when the Japanese get together privately to debrief themselves and plan their strategy for the next meeting that the experts speak up.

When Japanese experts have someone else on their team ask the questions, foreigners may conclude the negotiations without ever finding out who the experts are. When dealing with the Japanese, it does not always pay to display your *ude* up front.

> It is bad to carry even a good thing too far. Even concerning things such as Buddhism and moral lessons, talking too much will bring harm—*Tsunetomo Yamamoto (1569–1719), Samurai* (retired).

Practicing "Japaneseness"

It has been said that the only religion the Japanese have is being Japanese. On the surface, this statement may be true enough if you equate religion with belief in a certain economic ideology and a highly stylized social system that incorporates ritualistic practices designed to maintain and express both the belief and the system.

Japan's culture, which still today is codified, sanctified and ritualized to an extraordinary degree, homogenizes the Japanese to the point that, generally speaking, they often appear to have been cast from the same mold. This cultural conditioning, in both attitudes and physical behavior, is so pervasive that anyone who deviates from the national norm sticks out as if he or she were anti-matter.

Because of this conditioning in Japaneseness the Japanese are very sensitive to any attitude or action that does not conform to the national mold, and adherence to the national concept of Japaneseness is a prime principle. Individuals in the system are constantly monitoring the behavior of others as well as measuring themselves against all others. Much of this evaluating is automatic and subconscious, but it immediately becomes conscious and deliberate when any deviation is noted and when the situation calls for a judgment.

Because the Japanese tend to be clones of the same highly stylized and precisely formulated culture, they generally have a clear and comprehensive view of themselves—of what it means to be Japanese; that is, to think like and act like the model Japanese.

Not only are there precise guidelines for being Japanese, there are serious sanctions that can be and often are quickly and effectively applied against anyone who fails to live up to the established criteria for acceptable Japaneseness. The most common punishment is for the individual to loose his or her place in whatever group they are in.

One of the most popular and revealing of all such social gatherings designed to nurture Japaneseness is the *enkai* (inn-kigh), or banquet, traditionally staged in inns, restaurants or banquet halls—often in those that have Japanese style tatami-mat floors.

These banquets are microcosms of Japanese culture that demonstrate and reinforce virtually all of the forms of *kata-ized* behavior and speech that epitomize Japan's social system. It is at such gatherings that the Japanese bond with their friends and work groups and reaffirm their Japaneseness. It is there that their spirits are renewed and strengthened and their place in Japanese society confirmed.

Having participated in hundreds of such events myself, it appears to me that foreigners who have not had this experience, or are not able to fully join in the rituals that make up such meetings because of language and knowledge barriers are forever barred from full intimacy with Japanese culture.

Early in the 20th century, Japan's major trading companies recognized the importance of being able to understand and participate in the cultural rituals in countries where they had important interests. To cope with this challenge, they sent young traders abroad for two or three years for the specific purpose of learning the language and customs of the host country. They were not required, or expected, to do any work during this period.

This custom has gradually morphed into sending promising young managerial candidates abroad for post-graduate studies at famous business schools, such as the *Thunderbird Garvin School of International Management*, in Glendale, Arizona—my alma mater.

The importance of maintaining harmony in all relationships is of course a basic precept in human relations, but in most Western societies it ranges from weak to virtually non-existence. I believe there are lessons to be learned from Japan's samurai-influenced culture where it is both a conscious and subconscious effort that is ongoing, with a number of commonly recognized and used ritualistic type of methods for nurturing it.

The least that Americans in particular should do is incorporate in the educational system from day one through elementary school the teaching of a precise standard of etiquette and maintaining harmony in all relationships. This education should include specific ways for avoiding and resolving conflicts—all things obviously not taught in most homes today.

23

Samurai Style Sincerity

Bushi Gonomi no Makoto
(Buu-she Go-no-me no Mah-koh-toh)

One of the most important elements in the Bushido code, and one that has been totally integrated into the common culture of Japan, is conforming to the dictates of *seijitsu* (say-ee-jeet-sue), or *makoto* (mah-koh-toh), both of which translate as "sincerity, faithfulness, fidelity." The colloquial term *makoto* is more commonly used in ordinary speech.

Few if any foreigners doing business with Japanese could be accused of being insincere or unfaithful. But sincerity in English and *seijitsu* or *makoto* in Japanese are two different things, and therein lies the source of much of the friction and ill-will that can and does develop between foreigners and their Japanese counterparts.

Exercising sincerity in its Japanese sense means that one will behave in such a way that harmony is maintained, that nothing will be allowed to disrupt the relationship. This means faithfully fulfilling all of the obligations that are an integral part of the Japanese code of ethics, putting the interests of the group first, making no individual or arbitrary decisions, consulting with everyone on all matters; performing all of the personal/social rituals that make up the Japanese way.

Many Japanese who have had long experience dealing with Westerners are aware of the cultural differences inherent in their sense of sincerity, and they may personally make allowances to some degree. But generally they must abide by the cultural imperatives of their group and their company.

There is no perfect solution to this cultural difference, but foreigners who are aware of the differences can take a number of steps to avoid friction and breakdowns in the relationships. The first step is to be perfectly frank and upfront with the Japanese side, acknowledging that there may be differences in the way each side understands the relationship, and in the way the relationship is to proceed, and that you are prepared to discuss any matter that comes up and reach a satisfactory compromise.

Using this approach thereafter is a matter of anticipating differences in attitudes and approach, bringing them up and dealing with them in advance, and in reacting quickly to resolve any situation that arises before you can prevent it.

Problems frequently occur between Japanese and foreign companies because the foreign side fails to anticipate cultural differences, fails to explain their position fully, and fails to ask enough questions to fully understand where the Japanese are coming from. This latter syndrome is often a misplaced sense that asking such questions is impolite; that Japanese etiquette does not allow such behavior.

The Japanese, on the other hand, will typically ask questions, directly and indirectly, seemingly without end, especially during the early stages of a relationship.

The obvious point is that in order to achieve a truly sincere relationship, which both sides want, it is necessary to establish common grounds for pursuing the relationship. This generally entails compromises on both sides.

There have been occasions when foreign companies have made sincere and strong efforts to abide by all of the customs and rules of Japanese style *makoto* in business relationships. That is fine when the foreign side approves of the Japanese conducting the business in the Japanese way. If they do not fully accept the Japanese way of doing things, however, problems invariably arise.

Westerners must first be aware of the differences in the meaning of *makoto* and sincerity, and takes these into account with working out relationships with Japanese companies and in sustaining those relationships once they are underway. The best way to accomplish this is to write out in precise detail, as part of the agreement, the rules of sincerity they propose to follow.

The lesson to be learned from the *seijitsu* factor in Japanese culture is that it should be given as much priority in Western countries as in Japan, and that this priority be a conscious part of business, professional and personal relationships.

24

The Samurai Work Ethic

Bushi no Roudoh Rinri
(Buu-she no Roh-doh Reen-ree)

Midway through the Tokugawa Shogunate (1603–1868), it was formally taught that work should be regarded as a religious experience, and that work was the road to spiritual fulfillment.

The Japanese had no problem accepting this "new" economic theory because it was nothing more than formal recognition of something they had been practicing since the beginning of their civilization. The curriculum of this new school of thought came under the heading of *shikomu* (she-koe-muu), or "training in ethics and morality."

Shikomu remains a key element in the molding of the Japanese, not only in their academic schooling, but in their workplace training as well.

In fact, virtually all of the early indoctrination and training administered to new employees by Japan's large firms is in the *shikomu* of that particular company. Training in job performance comes second. Japanese employers recognize that, in the long run, beliefs and attitudes are more important than the manual skills new employees might bring into the firm, and that beliefs and attitudes often outweigh technical knowledge.

Shikomu is one of the "secrets" of the success of Japanese companies because it affects every facet of every enterprise, from the morale, the diligence, and the loyalty of employees to management-employee relations.

Back in the 1960s some Japanese companies began sending their new recruits to military style "boot camps," where they were drilled in how to work together, how to respond to superiors, and how to give their all for their companies, just like soldiers being trained to fulfill their role.

The new employees were trained to be formal and courteous in their speech, to not "horse around" while on the company premises, to take their duties and responsibilities seriously, and to keep their workplaces clean and well-ordered.

Still today, foreigners, particularly Americans, visiting Japan for the first time are invariably impressed, if not amazed, by the discipline and order they see in Japanese companies, including hotels and department stores.

Not surprisingly, Western influences are gradually undermining the role of *shikomu* in Japanese life. Even in the once strict school environment, the youth of Japan are more and more demonstrating the kind of attitudes and behavior one sees among children and teens in the United States and Europe.

However, Japanese must still conform to traditional behavioral patterns to a significant degree to get into Japan's better companies, and the *shikomu* system is so powerful that Japanese enterprises are not likely to shed their traditional skins any time soon.

Still, to maintain today's level of ethics and morality in Japanese culture it is imperative that the education system be returned to its earlier standards of good conduct and diligence, and this should be done before the last generations of "real" Japanese pass on—before it is too late.

Obviously, it behooves Western business, educational, and political leaders to integrate a high level of *shikomu* training in all school systems beginning with kindergarten. It is certainly not being done in a comprehensive way now.

25

Mutual Dependence

Sogo Izon
(Soh-goh Ee-zone)

Sogo izon (soh-goh ee-zone) or "mutual dependence" was a vital part of the samurai code of ethics, and in the post-samurai era was continued as a basic ingredient in families, in business and in society in general.

This concept, in its original form, has survived down to modern times, and continues to be a factor in the development of new businesses and in the growth of old ones, Japanese as well as foreign.

As is the case with many of Japan's culture-bound rules and customs, however, the *sogo izon* principle is not universal. It is applied selectively, both within Japan and in situations involving international interests. For example, small neighborhood stores selling toys were able to delay the entry of Toys R Us into Japan for several years by invoking the *sogo izon* concept and claiming that the practice of "mutual dependency" applied only to Japanese companies.

Japanese companies still base much of their personnel and business management on the principle of mutual dependency. This is most conspicuous in the interwoven relationships they develop with other companies and with various agencies of the government—all of which are designed to protect them from encroachers.

But in today's Japan mutual dependence to the degree that was traditional until the 1990s can be fatal to a company when it prevents rapid change and the rationalization of management to cope with national and international competition. The rise and fall of Nissan under its old management was a classic example of *sogo izon* taken to the extreme and petrified samurai attitudes that prevented change.

Now, the Japanese say that international *sogo izon* is an ideal they believe in and are working toward, and intellectually that is no doubt true. But on an emotional and spiritual level mutual international dependence is something that is difficult for them to accept, and will happen only over a relatively long period of time.

Western governments and corporations, working together, should create and implement precise, universal policies for mutual dependence on a global basis, rather than continue on the unclear, inexact and dangerous path now being followed.

26

The Word of a Samurai

Bushi no Ichi-gon
(Buu-she no Ee-chee-goan)

One of the primary tenets of the samurai code of ethics was to tell the truth and never go back on their word—a morality expressed in the phrase *bushi no ichi-gon*. *Bushi* (buu-she) means samurai or warrior; *ichi-gon* (ee-chee-goan) means one word; a single word. When used together they mean that the word of a samurai is as good as gold (to use a Western idiom).

Still today, most Japanese businessmen, especially those on a senior level, believe in and try to practice the concept of *bushi no ichigon*, which means that when they make a promise or commitment, they will keep it without any written contract or other formality.

Foreign businesspeople, diplomats and others can get a lot of mileage out of announcing to their Japanese counterparts that they want to do business the *bushi* way.

There are numerous anecdotal stories of the surprising honesty and integrity of Japanese businessmen. Some that I've heard involved money owed to American and European companies at the beginning of the Pacific War. The Japanese government banned all remittances to foreign accounts during the war years. When the war ended the money was still there and was soon paid to the proper recipients.

The word samurai, literally "one who serves," was already in use by the 9th century, when local warlords, most of whom were "extra" relatives of the royal family, began to retain the services of warriors, generally from among their kinsmen. By the 11th century, the samurai had become a distinct class, and the profession had become hereditary. In addition to fighting, the samurai also served their lords as managers and lesser officials. Tales of their loyalty to their lords are among the most extraordinary chronicles of Japanese history.

27

Sharing the Pain
in Bad Times

Fukeiki no Itami Wake
(Fuu-kay-ee-kee no Ee-tah-me Wah-kay)

The flip side of the Japanese penchant for cooperating and sharing the good among themselves is a firm belief that when there is pain, everyone should share that as well. This concept is expressed in the popular business term *itami wake* (ee-tah-me wah-kay), which literally means "dividing the pain." It goes back to the ancient government policy of collective responsibility, and became an integral part of the samurai code of ethics from the 13th century on.

Itami wake is commonly used in reference to sharing losses and disadvantages, whatever they may be, including disadvantages one party may have in negotiations. On such occasions, it is normal for the side that is being asked to give up the most expects the other side to share the pain. Among the Japanese, the stronger side in negotiations will frequently agree to *itami wake* without being asked, as a conspicuous, but not unexpected, goodwill gesture.

In the Japanese view, the willingness of Japanese management to share the pain of economic hard times by not firing employees as readily as foreign companies do, their preference for rigging bids to make sure all the key Japanese players get a piece of the action, and their advocacy of industry-wide price fixing to guarantee market stability, are all positive aspects of their *itami wake* philosophy.

One of the reasons why the Japanese traditionally opposed the proliferation of foreign companies in Japan was a deep-seated fear that they will cause market disruptions and other problems, because foreign companies did not subscribe to the *itami wake* ethic. The Japanese tend to see the *itami wake* way as uniquely Japanese, or as so little developed in other countries that foreign businesspeople lack the necessary "sincerity" to follow the practice.

Foreign businesspeople can, of course, offset some of the traditional suspicions and fears of their Japanese counterparts by announcing at the beginning of any relationship that they are familiar with the *itami wake* custom and that they are prepared to follow it when there are rational, fair, and legal reasons for doing so.

Letting your Japanese counterparts know you are aware of customs such as sharing the pain is a good way to earn credibility and to make them less likely to try to engage in unfair manipulations or other cultural ploys.

In times past, the Japanese tended to view their business relations with foreigners as combat, and some dregs of this attitude are still present. It is therefore often necessary—and always advisable—to put any business relationship on as personal a level as possible, and thereafter nurture it as one would a marriage.

The *itami wake* concept is one of the foundations of Western culture, but it does not square well with capitalism except in the form of corporate philanthropy and community service, which are already growing and could be raised to a higher level more rapidly, thus matching to some degree the Japanese *itami wake* approach.

28

Building Foundations of Trust

Shinyo ga Senketsu
(Sheen-yoh gah Sen-kate-sue)

There is probably no more important lesson that foreigners dealing with Japanese can learn than the importance of trust as exemplified by the Bushido code. In the code of the samurai, *shinyo* (sheen-yoh), or trust, was a tenuous thing that had to be constantly nurtured and reinforced by specific types of behavior. Failure to do this successfully always had serious consequences.

Shinyo was not easy to come by in feudal Japan. It had to involve numerous personal sacrifices and be built up over a relatively long period of time. But the efforts of the Japanese to live up to the standards of *shinyo* demanded by the samurai code resulted in the creation of a culture in which it was possible to trust people to do what was expected of them and to avoid any behavior that would disturb the harmony of society.

116   THE JAPANESE SAMURAI CODE

Of course, these standards were not always met, but they did result in the Japanese becoming more trustful, in things big and small, than what was achieved in other cultures. And this legacy of trustworthiness remains today one of the most important characteristics of the Japanese.

As mentioned elsewhere, the kind and degree of trust that has traditionally existed in Japan, and continues today as a significant factor, is the kind that makes it possible for businesses to place unprotected vending machines on the sidewalks without fearing that they will be vandalized and robbed; for shops to leave merchandise outside overnight and find it still there the following morning, for millions of people to leave bicycles at stations and find them there when they return.

Japanese want and need the kind and degree of trust implicit in *shinyo* in all of their dealings, but especially with foreigners because foreigners cannot automatically be trusted to fulfill all of the dictates of Japanese style trust.

It is, however, very important—and often absolutely necessary—that an acceptable level of trust be developed before the Japanese will commit to going into business with foreigners or a foreign company.

There are several elements that help to speed up the process of creating trust. The larger and older the foreign company, and the more positive its reputation, the more it is trusted. Foreign companies that have been successful in Japan are also automatically given some credit for being trustworthy. Small, unknown companies have to work much harder to achieve an acceptable level of trust.

It is on the personal side, the individuals concerned, that foreign companies most often encounter difficulty in establishing *shinyo* with Japanese. The cultural radar of the Japanese is always on, and it always scans every foreigner they come into contact with. In casual, informal situations this radar scan may operate in a very low mode. But in business situations it is on high.

The Japanese scan for age, sex, overall body appearance, the facial countenance, dress, physical behavior, manner of speech, and so on. In other words, they do a full *ninsomi* (nee-soh-me) or "body reading" scan, plus a behavioral scan.

If the scan reveals any negative elements—the person is too young, too aggressive, too brash, too talkative, talks too loud, has an unpleasant voice, does not have a kind face, does not have a sympathetic face, acts impatient—the individual is off to a poor start, and unless his or her looks and immediate behavior belies the character of an *iihito* (ee-ssh-toh), or "good person", it may be over before it starts.

In the Japanese context of things they initially put more stock in the people they deal with than in the company involved. Their reactions tend to be personal rather than based on principles or the objective reasoning preferred by Westerners. Establishing and maintaining trust on a personal basis is therefore especially important.

There is nothing mysterious about establishing a trust relationship with Japanese businesspeople. The way harks back to the positive side of the code of the samurai: never tell a lie, never fail to be courteous, never shame anyone, never disguise your intentions, never accept anything that is unfair or unreasonable, never display anger, never display weakness, never criticize your own company, always keep your word.

29

Accumulating Information

Jouho Shuushuu
(Joh-hoh Shuu-shuu)

Japan's history of seeking out and accumulating information from other countries goes back to the 6th century if not earlier, and reached a high mark in the 1870s when the government retained hundreds of authorities in business, education, finance, government, transportation and other categories from the U.S., Britain, Germany and other countries to help it transform Japan into an industrialized nation.

While the contracts with these foreign experts were limited to a few years, the Japanese continued to mine the world for knowledge and technology that would benefit their industry and their military from the 1870s until the beginning of the Pacific War in the early 1940s. But their obsession with importing foreign knowledge up to that time paled with what began around 1950.

Soon after the end of World War II in 1945 the U.S. began sponsoring fact-gathering tours for groups of Japanese in virtually all of the major industries, financing and escorting thousands of businesspeople to the U.S. and Europe on visits to banks, factories, farms, distribution centers, retail chains, etc.

By the mid–1950s the Japanese were arranging and financing their own trips abroad, and the number going overseas annually swelled to dozens of thousands. The Japan Productivity Center and the huge trading companies, Mitsui and Mitsubishi, were leaders in this mass effort.

By the end of the 1950s it was known in importing and exporting circles that Mitsubishi had one of the largest and most efficient worldwide information and intelligence gathering networks ever seen, and was widely regarded as more effective than the U.S.'s Central Intelligence Agency, the USSR's KGB, Britain's M-15, and later, Israel's Mossad.

The Japanese obsession with collecting information before initiating a project, and continuously thereafter, is in stark contrast to the behavior of many foreign companies, American firms in particular. Some foreign firms (not to mention government entities) still today do little and sometimes no research before initiating programs in Japan.

One facet of the Japanese compulsion to collect and use information from overseas is reflected in the book publishing industry. Virtually every business and technology related book published in the United States since the 1950s has been translated into Japanese and made available to the business community. The number is in the dozens of thousands.

In contrast to this, only a few dozen Japanese titles have been translated and published in English—not because there were so few good books that should have been made available in English, but because Western publishers were not aware that they existed, or did not see a market for them.

This Western myopia has improved slightly over the decades,

but the leaders in publishing Japanese translations today are Kodansha International, a Japanese company, and Tuttle Publishing Company, which was founded in Tokyo in 1948, is now part of the Periplus group based in Singapore, with major operations in Japan and the U.S.

30

Looking for "True Hearts"

Magokoro wo Motomete
(Mah-go-koh-roh oh Moh-toh-may-tay)

Another of Japan's cultural traits that evolved from the way of the samurai is the concept of putting as much or more emphasis on the character of individuals as on any practical talents they may have, or any other advantage a relationship with them might offer.

One of the things the Japanese both consciously and subconsciously look for in individuals they meet for the first time—especially if they are potential business partners on any level—is what is often described in Japanese terms as *magokoro* (mah-go-koh-roh), literally "true heart."

During the long samurai era the primary controls and sanctions that prescribed acceptable behavior were based on moral tenets; not laws. The few laws that existed were designed to protect and preserve the government; not the people.

Since the moral code by which common people lived was created and enforced by samurai, who were extraordinarily strict and quick to mete out harsh punishment, it was vital that the Japanese become paragons of *magokoro*, meaning that it was imperative for them to base their social, business and professional relationships on being scrupulously honest, sincere, trustworthy and dependable.

While the term *magokoro* is not used in everyday speech, it still provides the guidelines by which the Japanese evaluate potential business and professional partners. In fact, business relationships are seen as moral relationships—a viewpoint that is not exactly alien to Westerners, but is certainly not at the forefront of their decision-making or conduct.

Westerners can significantly improve the potential of developing a successful relationship with a Japanese company, organization or government entity by letting their counterparts know up front that they want the relationship to be based on *magokoro*.

Given the corporate scandals in Japan, in the U.S. and elsewhere in the 1990s and beyond, it would seem to go without saying that all education institutions worldwide should incorporate the concept of *magokoro* into their programs.

31

Looking for a Third Eye

Dosatsu Ryoku (Daisan no Me) wo Sagasu
(Doh-sot-sue Rio-kuu (Die-sahn no may) oh Sah-gah-sue)

A long time ago yoga masters in India and later Zen Buddhist monks China, Korea and Japan used meditation and introspection to achieve a level of knowledge and wisdom that went well beyond the observable physical world.

As already mentioned, an Indian master learned that the blood circulates through the body by introspection more than a thousand years before European physicians figured it out. Asian history is replete with other examples of other planes of existence and knowledge.

Japan's samurai used Zen techniques to develop their senses far beyond what is ordinary, especially their ability to hear and their ability to perceive things that could not be seen.

One aspect of this extraordinary ability is expressed in the term *dosatsu ryoku* (doh-sot-sue rio-kuu), which may be translated "as the ability to see through things, insight, penetration, see into the future," or what I refer to as "a third eye."

While only a small percentage of Japan's present-day businesspeople and professionals engage in Zen techniques in an effort to develop a "third eye," the majority nevertheless attempt to use this ability on the basis of the combined cultural skills they have inherited.

When top Japanese business leaders are called upon to evaluate younger executive for promotion, especially those who are on track to become executives, directors and presidents, they look for people who have demonstrated that they have *dosatsu-ryoku*.

Westerners seem to regard an MBA as a "third eye," but there are fundamental differences in what MBA candidates learn in school and in what can be learned through tapping into a higher power. It seems to me that all managers and executives would benefit from studying Zen as a life philosophy as well as to enhance their business skills.

Some corporations send their trainees as well as their managers and executives to private Zen schools, where they study Zen techniques and business-oriented practices that are impregnated with Zen. Other employees are sent to public temples. An impressive number of Japanese businesspeople voluntarily attend Zen sessions in nearby temples.

32

The Do or Die Factor

Inochigake no Seichin
(Ee-no-chee-gah-kay no Say-ee-cheen)

One of the most conspicuous characteristics of the Bushido code that is alive and well in contemporary Japan is expressed in the term *gambari* (gahm-bah-ree), a derivative of one of the "Four Gs" introduced earlier, which means to never give up, to persevere against all odds, to do or die in the attempt.

The samurai of Shogunate era Japan were physically, mentally and spiritually drilled in the concept of *gambari*—as were the soldiers and other military forces of pre-World War II Japan—and while the power of the spirit of *gambari* has diminished considerably in contemporary Japan it remains strong enough that it distinguishes the Japanese from many other people.

In fact, the diligence and the perseverance of present-day Japanese is one of the most significant and important legacies of Bushido.

Gambari has several meanings, including being patient in the pursuit of one's goals, but the most important one today is the idea of working hard; first to look good in the eyes of one's group and to one's superiors, and second to contribute to the success of Japan—a nationalistic element that has its roots in the spirit of the samurai, who saw themselves as the embodiment of Japan.

Gambari is one of the most used words in the vocabulary of the Japanese, and is something like a national mantra. It is used in the daily conversation of athletes, businessmen, entertainers, factory workers, managers, school children, etc.—every category of people in the country—to express their intention of never giving up in their efforts to achieve something.

Isshokenmei (ees-show-kane-may-ee) is another term that is indicative of the positive character of the Japanese. Its original meaning was "to guard a place with one's life," and no doubt came into use because people were required to stake their lives on their behavior during the samurai era.

Today the term is always used in the phrase *isshokenmei yarimasu* (ees-show-kane-may-ee yah-ree-mahss), which is the equivalent of "I will do my best," and is also very much like a national mantra.

Of course, the old connotation of staking one's life is still inherent in the use of *isshokenmei*, and the word remains characteristic of the Japanese attitude and approach to things. It has the connotation of giving one's all, and is almost like taking an oath.

Foreign businesspeople interacting with their Japanese counterparts can judiciously use *isshokenmei yarimasu* to emphasize their commitment to a relationship or project. It resonates deeply in the Japanese soul.

Still another aspect of the Japanese character that is out of the book of the samurai, and has played a major role in Japan's success, is expressed in the phrase *akiramenai* (ah-kee-rah-may-nigh), literally, "I can't give up."

For centuries the Japanese were programmed to persevere in whatever they set out to do, regardless of the obstacles and hardships they encountered. This conditioning was so thorough that perseverance became automatic. *Akiramenai* became a byword, and not being able to give up permeated the psyche of the Japanese.

The characteristic persistence of the Japanese, whether in pursuing artistic skills, martial arts, business or other goals is partly rooted in the *akiramenai* factor, with unbounded pride also playing a key role.

Although the power of Japan's "do or die" cultural conditioning has been steadily declining since the end of the feudal system in 1945, it was so strong and pervasive for so long that the legacy lingers on, and still today the characteristic is readily discernible in the behavior of most adult Japanese.

Among many Westerners, on the other hand, the do-or-die philosophy is altogether missing where work is concerned, meaning that it is not a comprehensive cultural trait. As also previously noted, in the West it is likely to be seen in its purest form in sports and in other selected areas where the stakes are high and success is based on individuals competing against each other.

Common sense tells us there is a time to give up and walk away from situations that are obviously doomed to failure, or when it becomes clear that the benefits will not justify the effort. But just as obviously, an injection of the do-or-die spirit into many Western and Middle Eastern cultures could be of enormous help to humanity.

Determination is more important than wisdom or talent—
Tsunetomo Yamamoto (1659–1719), Samurai.

33

The Fighting Spirit Factor

Konjo no Yohso
(Kone-joh no Yoh-soh)

During the Shogunate era young males in the samurai class were pro-grammed to an incredible degree to possess unwavering courage, achieve extraordinary skill with the sword and other weapons, be absolutely fearlessness, and have a disdain for death that was sublime in its essence.

These characteristics were subsumed in the term *konjo* (kone-joh), which translates as "fighting spirit," and incorporates the con-cepts of determination and tenacity. This fighting spirit played a significant role in Japan's transformation from the devastation of World War II to the world's second largest economy in less than thirty years, and although now far less visible than what it was dur-ing those decades, it continues to be an important facet of the Japanese character.

Japanese companies today continue to look for entry-level employees who have displayed strong *konjo* during their school careers, and this is the reason high school and university athletes, especially those who played soccer, are in such demand.

Overall, the Japanese are still culturally programmed to succeed in whatever they set out to do. Their determination and focus continues to pay off in technological advances in many fields. The number of patents issued annually to individual Japanese, research organizations and corporations puts them in contention with the United States as being the most inventive people on the planet—which is astounding, given the fact that until industrialization was imposed on Japan from the top in the 1870s and 80s innovation and invention were taboo.

One of Japan's major challenges today is to come up with a new educational system that promotes the *konjo* spirit in a humane and rational way.

By the same token, there are lessons to be learned from the traditional *konjo* of the Japanese that Westerners should not ignore.

The fighting spirit of the samurai was honed to a high degree by their years of hard, serious training, which in earlier times often resulted in death. In peacetime as well as war, it was the custom for individual samurai to engage in one-on-one duels to the death with warriors from other schools and other areas. *Ronin* (roh-neen) samurai, those without masters, frequently hired themselves out as guards, and sometimes as assassins, and were thus in constant danger.

34
The Lavish Use of Energy

Oshiminaku Ki wo Tsukau
(Oh-she-me-nah-kuu Kee oh T'sue-kow)

Until 1870 life in Japan did not require an unceasing, abundant use of energy. Living was relatively slow-paced and coordinated with the seasons. From the late 1600s until the end of the Tokugawa Shogunate in 1868 the mass of samurai warriors (who were not allowed to work at regular jobs) and the townspeople had lots of leisure time, which they spent in artistic and recreational activities. Many people traveled around the country on foot, spending weeks to months on the road on religious pilgrimages, sightseeing, and some just for the adventure of it.

In fact, by 1650 there were specific laws preventing projects and other activities that would have changed the economy and the pace of living.

But all of this changed within two years after the fall of the Tokugawa Shogunate in 1868. The government mandated changes that transformed the country from a farming and handcraft economy to a modern industrial economy in just twenty years. This transformation succeeded because of what the Japanese call *ki wo tsukao* (kee oh t'suu-kow) or "the use of energy."

But the full sense of this phrase can be understood only when it is related to the breadth and depth of the changes that occurred in Japan's economy and lifestyle between 1870 and 1890. It was an astounding example of what organized human effort can achieve in a very short time.

An even greater level of *ki* was unleashed a second time following Japan's defeat in World War II, with results that were even more astounding.

Ki refers to both emotional and spiritual energy, which was suppressed in Japan during the reign of the samurai and channeled into a very narrow way of life that resulted in some remarkable achievements in the arts and crafts. But it left the Japanese with an unused reservoir of energy and emotion that was like a bomb waiting to explode.

Present-day Japanese society, which is still colored by the legacy of the Bushido code, still requires the use of extraordinary amounts of emotional and psychic energy—far more than is needed in the U.S., for example, because of the requirements of etiquette and far more intense competition.

The challenge for the Japanese is to dispense with the etiquette and other cultural behavior that require great amounts of *ki* and hinder rather than contribute to the conduct of business and politics, and to use the emotion and energy in positive, beneficial ways.

The challenge for the West is to become more aware of the existence and the role that *ki* plays in business and other endeavors, and to learn how to focus its power far more effectively.

35

The Power of Kanji

Kanji no Chikara
(Kahn-jee no Chee-kah-rah)

All Japanese have a sense of form, balance and spatial harmony that verges on the professional, thanks to the physical and mental training they undergo in the process of learning how to draw the *Kanji* (Kahn-jee) or ideograms, that make up their way of writing.

Kanji, which means "Chinese characters," were developed in China several thousand years ago, introduced to the Korean peninsula over two thousand years ago, and brought from Korea to Japan between the 5th and 6th centuries A.D..

The *Kanji* originated as drawings of the things they represented, and are made up of one to twenty-five or more lines or strokes. Early Chinese dictionaries contained some 50,000 characters, a number that was gradually reduced over the centuries.

Until the end of the 19th century, well educated Japanese had to learn how to read and write some 5,000 characters to be literate. In the 1980s this number was reduced to 1,945, plus an additional 200 or so that appear only in names.

Buddhism was the primary vehicle for the introduction of *Kanji* into Japan because the literature of Buddhism was written in the characters. And just as they adopted the basic characters themselves, the Japanese also adopted the Chinese custom of drawing the ideograms as an art form.

Over time, skill in drawing the *Kanji* as art forms, known as *Shodo* (Show-doh), "The Way of Writing" became so important in its cultural context that it came to be equated with morality as well as the mark of an educated person. Those who became exceptionally skilled won lasting fame, and are still honored today.

Not only did Buddhist monks and scholars strive to become masters of the art of *Shodo*. It became a basic part of the education and training of samurai. The meanest warrior was expected to have the skill of an artist in drawing the characters.

The process of learning how to draw the *Kanji* begins in kindergarten and continues for several years. There is a prescribed order of the strokes that must be combined into an ideogram that is not only readable but also has enough artistic merit to meet a basic standard.

Few Japanese today become *Shodo* masters, but the training nevertheless has a fundamental influence on the manual dexterity of the Japanese, as well as on their recognition and appreciation of forms and relationships in general.

This training from childhood is a significant element in the ability of the Japanese to create attractive designs and to accomplish tasks that require hand-and-eye coordination in dealing with small, complex things.

I am not going to suggest that Westerners take up the practice of *Kanji*, but requiring all students to develop a high level of penmanship would have a positive impact on their character and on their approach to life in general.

36

Knowing Without Being Told

Anmoku no Ryokai
(Ahn-moh-kuu no Rio-kigh)

Because of their cultural homogeneity, the Japanese have a set of common values and a body of common knowledge, traditionally referred to as *anmoku no ryokai* (ahn-moh-kuu no rio-kigh), or "unspoken understanding," that gives them an advantage in their dealings among themselves as well as with foreign businesspeople and politicians.

Generally speaking, this *anmoku no ryokai* factor means that in any encounter with foreigners, a group of Japanese presents a solid team front, unified by their cultural conditioning, that makes them formidable opponents. Each member of the group knows how the other members are going to react. They have specific roles to play, and play them according to their cultural script.

Foreigners dealing with the Japanese are often handicapped

because they have been conditioned in the opposite way—to think and behave as individuals. It goes without saying that when facing a well-trained team in sports, business, or politics, the only recourse is to field a team that is equally if not better trained, which is a lesson that many Western companies and countries have yet to learn.

Another facet of Japanese culture that was refined and spread by the samurai can be described as things that are *atarimae* (ah-tah-ree-my). *Atarimae* means "natural, proper, reasonable, common, normal" and is used in reference to attitudes, ideas and behavior that is expected; that is taken for granted and doesn't require discussion or explanation.

These *atarimae* attitudes and things became the Japanese mindset, "The Japanese Way," passed on from one generation to the next, primarily through observation and imitation.

Still today, new white-collar employees are expected to learn most of what they need to know without being told. Westerners are always asking why and how. It is common for Japanese to remain quiet and watch. Another aspect of this situation is that traditionally in Japanese culture asking questions was considered rude, and admitting ignorance of anything resulted in loss of face. Silence was therefore the better part of valor.

Dealing with the *atarimae* factor in Japan can be a subtle and difficult challenge for Westerners. Just as Westerners tend to automatically assume that logic, fairness, and mutual benefit will carry the day, the Japanese automatically tend to take the position that any foreign refusal to accept their terms results from the fact that the foreign side does not understand how the Japanese see and do things—a cultural myopia that is even more characteristic of Americans, if that is possible.

The lesson to be learned here is that Americans and other Westerners—and the Japanese, too—must be weaned from their cultural blindness. Obviously, what is *atarimae* in one culture may not be in another.

The ultimate challenge, of course, is to raise the standards of behavior and product quality worldwide to the maximum possible, and make those standards *atarimae*.

37

Programming the Body

Karada de Oboeru
(Kah-rah-dah day Oh-boh-eh-rue)

It might be said that the first commandment in the rule book of Bushido is that skill in any art or craft begins with training the body to act in a certain way. Fledgling samurai practiced the techniques of sword-fighting several hours a day for many years. Their goal was to reach the point where their bodies assimilated the movements in a process that was called *karada de oboeru* (kah-rah-dah day oh-boh-eh-ruu), or "learning with the body."

The most dedicated samurai attempted to reach a transcendent level in which their bodies performed the techniques perfectly without them having to think about what they were doing.

In simple terms, the *karada de oboeru* process consisted of repeating physical actions on an increasingly difficult level until they became automatic—the same approach used by master musicians, jugglers, typists and others, who perform flawlessly, seemingly without conscious effort.

Over the centuries, *karada de oboeru* became the underlying foundation for all of the arts and skills practiced in Japan, from such mundane things as weaving baskets and floor mats to writing. But it was in the martial arts and higher fine arts that *karada de oboeru* made its major contributions, allowing the more dedicated of these artists to achieve skills verging on the sublime.

Because of the overall role and importance of the *karada de oboeru* concept in Japanese life, it eventually permeated the thinking and behavior of people in business. Succeeding in business was seen as a matter of combining spirit and physical effort. In other words, work hard enough and long enough and with enough spirit, and anything can be accomplished.

The *karada de oboeru* concept is still visible today in the management philosophies and practices of larger Japanese companies. Dedication and spirit still rank higher than talent. Years of laboring away in on-the-job experience is still seen as the best way for developing the human relations-oriented managerial skills prized in Japanese companies.*

The Japanese naturally believe that their particular *karada de oboeru* method of training is superior to all other methods, and they tend to look down on people who do not have the awareness, ambition, or stamina, to accept and follow their approach.

---

* Masao Ogura, founder and chief builder of Yamato Transport Co., with its famous logo of a mother cat carrying a baby cat in its mouth, was noted for his leadership philosophy, which would be at home in any Western company (logical thinking, keeping up with the trends of the times, strategic thinking, proactive management, self-reliant spirit, no bureaucracy, no dependence on politicians, good media relations, a cheerful personality, always pay your own way, and high ethical standards). But he ordained that promotions in the hugely successful company be based on character, not performance.

38

The Perfect Mind-Body Meld

Mushin/Muga
(Muu-sheen/Muu-gah))

The secret of the extraordinary skill with the sword and other weapons that the samurai developed was a result of combining physical, mental and spiritual training over a period of many years—something that outstanding athletes, artists and others have done for ages.

The ultimate in such training is to achieve a state of *mushin* (muu-sheen), or "no mind", so that the mind does not interfere with the body in performing what it has been trained to do. Another term for this state of mind [mentioned earlier] is *muga* (muu-gah), which means "without ego." *

Few Japanese today are trained to the point that they achieve a constant state of *muga*, but many go far enough that they are able to achieve extraordinary things in the arts and crafts and in the design and production of other products.

Neither do all Japanese businesspeople hie to a Zen temple or monastery to hone their *muga* skills. Some do it with kendo, others with archery. One of the friends of expatriate manager and scuba devotee James Fink does it by spending thirty minutes under water in his scuba gear before approaching the task of designing a new product.

One does not have to reach a state of complete *muga* to derive benefits. The effort itself results in relieving stress, clearing the mind, stilling the spirit and bringing harmony to the mind-body relationship.

Ex-CEO, author and management consultant Michihiro Matsumoto points out that the fundamental secret of any special skills and talents that the Japanese have is a product of discipline—mental and physical discipline to the point that they are able to "lose" their conscious self and perform whatever action they are taking perfectly—a principle that is right out of the book of the samurai.

"Once you have reached this state of body-mind meld you don't have to think about what you are doing," Matsumoto says. "It becomes an automatic response to your will. You don't have to analyze or be struck by doubts. You just do it!"

This, of course, is something that great athletes, artists, craftsmen and masters in other fields have always done. The big differ-

---

*   Says Japan-educated journalist-author Glenn Davis, "One of the biggest benefits for a Westerner seeking wisdom from Bushido is learning how to suppress one's ego and individuality. This is probably as relevant today as 100 years ago, if not more so. Westerners spend so much of their energy posturing and polishing their over-sized egos, wasting energy that could be used toward more productive ends. Japanese spiritualism and Bushido put much emphasis on the intuitive part of the brain, something that could be useful in teaching and training methods in the West, if it were better understood. If Western businessmen could stop rolling their eyes long enough to discard their prized logic, intuitive learning *a la Japanois* could follow. This could be taught in Western schools, as an "alternative" method of analysis.

ence where Japan is concerned is that this level of discipline became an integral part of the common culture, and remains a powerful influence.

Matsumoto, who is also Japan's leading debate advocate, teaches that to master any art one must meld thought and feeling the way the warrior becomes one with his sword. The form of *Eigo-do* (Aa-ee-go doh), or "The Way of English", that he teaches is based on the same principle. He says that you must practice until it is "the English speaking, not you!" He adds that to master the language you must "become English!"

These concepts, too, are pure Bushido.

I have been advocating for decades that kendo or karate be made an integral part of the education and training of all children throughout the world, and that it be continued throughout life. Both kendo and karate include training the mind as well as the body, and exemplify discipline, self-control, self-confidence, and respect for others. The rewards would be enormous.

39

Managing from the Belly

Haragei
(Hah-rah-gay-ee)

One of the most remarkable and intriguing aspects of Japanese culture is the ongoing prevalence and importance of nonverbal communication. By the end of the Heian period in Japanese history in 1192, when the shogunate government was founded, the prevailing philosophy, etiquette and life-style of the upper-class had become so homogenized that it was possible for people to practically "read" each other's minds.

From around the 14th century, Zen priests began promoting a method of communication—much of it non-verbal—that came to be called *haragei* (hah-rah-gay-ee), or "the art of the stomach." *Hara* means "stomach", *gei* means "an art."

The samurai quickly adopted *haragei* as the purist and ultimate form of communication. Its perceived validity was based on the concept that the stomach was the site of the soul and spirit, and was therefore the truest source of communication.

The actual ability to communicate via *haragei* came with the physical, mental and spiritual training undergone by the samurai, combined with age and experience.

In the Western context, *haragei* is often expressed as "gut feelings" or "intuition." "Common sense" also incorporates aspects of *haragei*. In Japan, however, it went much further than what these terms connote because it was recognized and practiced as a legitimate form of communication.

In his book, *Haragei: The Unspoken Way*, Michihiro Matsumoto [who has patterned his life after that of Musashi Miyamoto, Japan's greatest sword fighter] defines *haragei* as a way of influencing and controlling others on the basis of the traditional Japanese cultural mindset, and is a demonstration of unbounded self-confidence and courage.

Matsumoto also explains *haragei* as the act of dealing with people or situations through ritual formalities and accumulated, shared cultural experience, including *amae* (presuming upon the goodwill of others), *tatemae* (a verbal façade presented to conceal one's true thoughts or intentions) and *honne* (one's true thoughts and intentions).

Like so many other facets of Zen Buddhism and Bushido that have survived into modern times, *haragei* is still a "tool" of many Japanese who depend upon it to guide them in making business and other important decisions.

The late businessman Konosuke Matsushita, founder of the Matsushita empire, was considered a master of *haragei*, as were the founders and first managers of most of Japan's great companies, including Toyota, Sony and Honda.

Because Japan is a high content culture in which people ask few questions, value silence and prefer teaching by example, *haragei* was, and is, virtually indispensable in judging the character and managing others. Older businessmen in particular pride themselves on their skill in using *haragei*.

Saying that a person has *hara* means that he is broad-minded and magnanimous, pays no attention to details, and has an intangible "presence" that enables him to influence others by doing nothing. At the same time, the man with *hara* must also be seen as a man with an abundance of *toku* (toh-kuu), or virtue, in order for others to support and follow him.

Another key term in the cultural vocabulary of Japan that is closely related to *haragei* is *ishin denshin* (ee-sheen dane-sheen), which is translated as tacit understanding and is what I call "cultural telepathy."

All Japanese, especially older people in positions of authority, make constant use of *ishin denshin* in interacting with others because their shared cultural knowledge, experiences and conditioning make it possible for them to virtually "read" other people's minds.

Since Westerners, Americans in particular, are on a totally difficult cultural wavelength than the Japanese they have difficulty tuning in to Japanese thinking, and generally cannot predict Japanese behavior. By the same token, without significant exposure to Western cultures, Japanese are typically unable to predict Western behavior, and consider Americans the most unpredictable people of all because of our individualistic way of thinking and acting.

The best way for inexperienced Western businesspeople and others to deal with *haragei* and the attendant cultural traits is to inform the Japanese up front that you realize you are on different cultural channels and that will do you utmost to help find a middle channel where you both understand what the other is thinking, needs and wants.

Westerners, even Americans, have a degree of cultural intuition that they use daily, generally without being aware of it. It would be wise for us to consciously recognize the role and importance of cultural-based *haragei*, and like the Japanese, make it an integral part of our educational process, incorporating all of the most desirable and admirable human traits.

40

The Harmonious Way
of Doing Business

Nemawashi no Bijinesu Yarikata
(Nay-mah-wah-she no Be-jee-nay-suu Yah-ree-kah-tah)

The dictates of harmony and maintaining the imperatives of the hierarchical system required by the Bushido code of ethics made it essential during the samurai era that the Japanese be very circumspect and follow prescribed ways in achieving consensus and making decisions.

This cultural imperative, only slightly diminished in today's Japan, is typically achieved through a process known as *nemawashi* (nay-mah-wah-she), mentioned earlier, which originally meant "revolving the roots" when transplanting something, but now means informal behind-the-scenes discussions involving some action or decision that someone wants to initiate.

The process of *nemawashi* requires that the person or people who originated the proposed action meet individually with all of the people who would be directly involved, with the goal of getting their support prior to a group meeting where the proposal must be formally approved before it can be initiated.

If the *nemawashi* has been successful, the group meeting is more or less ceremonial—very much like a diplomatic agreement that has been reached in advance by underlings and finally goes to top officials for their signature.

The *nemawashi* process requires dealing with a number of individuals who have their own agendas and concerns and is therefore generally time-consuming, but by getting all of the key individuals onboard before initiating a project the possibility for its success is greatly enhanced. As I've stated elsewhere, Americans make decisions about new projects in minutes or hours, and then take months to a year or more to get the understanding and cooperation necessary to begin the programs. By doing *nemawashi* in advance [which can take months to a year!], the Japanese are able to initiate projects the day they are formally approved.

Foreign newcomers to Japan who are not aware of the *nemawashi* process are often frustrated by the apparent lack of activity regarding their proposals. Learning how *nemawashi* works and becoming skilled in the process is one of the primary keys to doing business successfully with Japanese.

Many foreign companies have already adapted this traditional Japanese approach to vetting and initiating new programs. I recommend that the *nemawashi* process be made a part of the basic education of everyone, because it works in any situation where decisions that affect others are to be made.

41

The Advantage of Fuzzy Thinking

Aimai no Bigaku
(Aye-my no Bee-gah-kuu)

Until the end of the Tokugawa Shogunate in 1868 Japan's samurai government enforced a culture that prohibited thinking and acting outside of a closed box. But, the ending of the Shogunate form of government did not let most Japanese out of the box. That did not happen until 1945, at the end of World War II, when for the first time in the history of the country large numbers of Japanese had the freedom to think and act on their own, to experiment and to innovate.

The Japanese had virtually no practical experience with intellectual or physical freedom, but thanks to their samurai code of ethics they had exceptionally keen minds, a very practical way of looking at things, limitless pride, and limitless confidence in their ability to do anything they set out to do.

They also had other advantages. First, they were not saddled with age-old conventions and restraints when it came to adapting Western technology. Second, they had been endowed by their culture with the ability to discern the essence of new products and concepts; to see them unencumbered by cultural baggage, and to improve on them by eliminating or reducing the non-essentials.

And finally, their Shinto and Buddhist training had given them the ability to look at things holistically—taking into consideration variables and things that are often not obvious or visible to linear thinkers. They were, in other words, naturally "fuzzy thinkers"— something that became increasingly advantageous to them as the world moved into the computer age. [The fuzzy thinking concept has been referred to by some Japanese authorities as "soft logic."]

This "third eye" ability made it possible for the Japanese to be the first to take advantage of "fuzzy thinking," an approached first developed by an American but virtually ignored in the U.S. until the Japanese demonstrated its value in practical situations.

In 1986 Japan's Ministry of International Trade and Industry (MITI) made the holistic use of technology the official policy of the government. MITI labeled its concept *yugoka* (yuu-go-kah), which translates as the "fusion" of ideas and technologies, as opposed to mixing them.

MITI explained that combining two technologies does not change the essence of their individual natures, while the fusion of different technologies transforms them into something entirely new.

Actually, Japanese researchers were already using the *yugoka* principle before MITI issued its White Paper because it was natural for them to think in such terms. But making the principle government policy contributed to a growing flood of technological innovations and breakthroughs that have since become the foundation of Japan's industries, from electronics to biology.

The *yugoka* principle, which is based on holistic or fuzzy thinking, is, of course, known in the West and is used by a growing number of scientists and others. But only the surface of its power has been tapped. The principle, which can be directly applied to cultural, economic, political scientific, social and other situations, should be introduced into the basic education systems worldwide.

42
Adjusting to Change

Henka ni Taiou
(Hane-kah nee Tie-oh-uu)

A long time ago, the Japanese accepted the idea that the world at large is in a constant state of flux and that, under the circumstances, the best philosophy of life is one based on flexibility—on being able to bend with the wind.

Despite the fact that the Japanese were programmed for centuries by the code of the samurai to think and behave in precise, absolute ways and to resist change—something that remains today in the mindset of too many government bureaucrats, and some of the professions—they nevertheless harbored an inherent ability to change their focus and their ways at a moment's notice, both when *jijo henko* (jee-joh hane-koh), which means changed or changing circumstances, demanded it, and when they had the opportunity to do so on their own free will.

One of the areas where Westerners and Japanese have encountered friction is in their view and use of contracts. Written contracts were virtually unheard of in Japan until the industrialization and Westernization of the economy between 1870 and 1890. Westerners tend to look upon contracts as cast in stone. In Japan, on the other hand, agreements were traditionally verbal and open-ended, allowing for regular adjustments that could be initiated by either side when their circumstances change. In the samurai mentality, their word was better than any written agreement.

A samurai's word is harder than metal—*samurai code of ethics*.

When the Western practice of written contracts was introduced into Japan, the Japanese tended to look upon them as evidence that Westerners were so unethical and immoral that they did not trust themselves or anyone else to keep their word. The Japanese also regarded the idea of being forced to abide by a detailed contract as irrational and ridiculous, because there was no way that any situation could remain the same for either party over a period of time.

However, by the 1970s most Japanese companies had become resigned to the idea of signing contracts with foreign partners, but they did not give up on the concept of *jijo henko*, and generally they continued to interpret the contracts they signed as being only guidelines, subject to revision as the circumstances warranted.

In the decades since, and during which time the Japanese have become much more heavily involved in business overseas, the Japanese have developed a new appreciation of Western-style contracts in their international affairs. At home, however, the Japanese still tend to regard the contracts they sign as being "adjustable."

Japanese see no contradiction in their unilateral treatment of contracts. When they reinterpret contracts the other side is expected to understand and accept their actions even if it inconveniences them and costs money. [This is the *amae* principle in action.] It is understood in such situations that the side "breaking" the contract owes the other side a similar indulgence in the future, so that in the end everything will balance out—a very Buddhist concept.

Foreigners going into contractual arrangements with Japanese companies should be aware of the *jijo henko* factor in Japanese thinking and avoid unpleasant surprises by staying in constant contact with their partners, officially as well as unofficially. Unofficial contact refers to after-hours meetings in casual and recreational situations, because it is usually in these settings that Japanese reveal what is going on behind the scenes.

In the past, and still today to an alarming degree, Americans in particular have tended to regard the signing of a contract with a Japanese (or Chinese or Korean!) company as the end of the hard work. In reality, negotiating a contract is the easy part. The demanding part comes with keeping the relationship on a harmonious path through constant adjustments—like a surfer on a surfboard.

One of the primary reasons why such constant adjustment of contracts worked so well in Japan, and why it is still a common practice, is because of the legacy of honesty, loyalty, and goodwill the Japanese inherited from Bushido.

I do not recommend that foreigners doing business in Japan (or elsewhere in Asia) dispense with contracts, but it is very important that they understand how the Japanese and other Asians perceive written agreements, and develop skill in dealing with the *jijo kenko* concept.

43

Harmonious Reconciliation

Wakai
(Wah-kigh)

There are, of course, major cultural factors involved in the way the Japanese react to disputes, all of them evolving from the system of justice created by the country's samurai ruling class generations ago.

A key factor in the approach to law enforcement in Japan is an expectation that both parties to any dispute will compromise their positions to the point that they can reach a settlement before the case goes to trial—a process known as *wakai* (wah-kigh), which translates as "reconciliation" or "harmonious dissolution."

There were many reasons for the popularity of *wakai* in feudal Japan. One important reason was that it was the custom to treat both parties to a dispute as guilty. The rationale was simple. It takes two people to quarrel or fight. Making both parties subject to punishment was a powerful incentive for people to avoid confrontations that could come to the attention of the authorities.

Another reason for *wakai* was that punishment in pre-modern Japan tended to be collective. That is, the family and sometimes the whole community of a criminal or a suspect were often treated as equally guilty and subject to punishment.

One of the most famous case of collective responsibility and punishment occurred during the early decades of the Tokugawa Shogunate (1603–1868) when a farmer named Sogo went over the head of his local lord and handed the Shogun a petition seeking redress from the high taxes imposed on farmers in the fief. The Shogun sent investigators to the domain, and subsequently ordered the fief lord to lower the taxes. But the local lord had his revenge by having Sogo, his wife, and his two young sons beheaded for embarrassing him.

Just as in feudal times, most Japanese courts require that the parties to a disagreement bring in substantial evidence that they have tried to settle the dispute themselves before the courts will agree to accept the case. As a result of these cultural factors, most disputes in Japan are resolved by mediation, either directly between the parties concerned, or through a mediator. There are professional mediators who belong to the Japan Association of Mediators, which publishes a guide called *A Handbook of Mediation*.

Foreign individuals and companies in Japan are well advised to make use of mediators and arbiters in any case they might become involved in, whether it concerns something as mundane as a dispute with a landlord, or one as serious as an accident that results in death or a criminal charge.

Americans and other Westerners are generally conditioned to think in terms of the letter of the law. The Japanese, on the other hand, regard the law as a last resort, and think of laws as suggested guidelines.

Japan's samurai had another attitude that might be very wise for Westerners to emulate. They believed that the more laws a government has on the books the less law-abiding people will be…a lesson taught by Confucius nearly three thousand years ago. [Lawmakers in the U.S. take notice!]

A more basic concept in the Japanese art of compromising is subsumed in the twin terms *gohjo* (gohh-joh), cooperation, and *gojoh* (goh-johh), compromise. Together the two terms refer to compromising one's own desires or demands in order to cooperate in a mutually beneficial relationship—a concept deeply embedded in Japanese culture by the combination of Buddhism and Bushido.

Misunderstandings and friction frequently result between Japanese and foreigners attempting to establish a professional relationship because of different cultural conceptions of the meaning of compromise.

Gojoh goes well beyond a trade-off that is controlled by a sense of fairness, equality, goodwill, and mutual trust. It includes a strong personal element that revolves around mutual friends, mutual interests, and common goals, and often results in a relationship being very lopsided, but mutually acceptable.

When evaluating a potential business relationship, the Japanese generally look for the personal element first—the attitudes and behavior of the individuals they meet, and how they read their character. This is vital to them because any relationship inevitably calls for cooperation and compromise to keep it going smoothly, and the character and personality of the individuals involved is key to this process.

Internationally oriented businesspeople in Japan are gradually absorbing the Western concept of an objective approach to corporate relationships. But they cannot eliminate all of the personal and emotional aspects of their culture without losing the ability to function effectively in their own country.

Probably the biggest complaint that the Japanese have had about the corporate culture of America since U.S. firms began showing up in Japan is that it is not personal or emotional enough; that it treats people inhumanely.

Since the 1990s economic factors have forced the Japanese to partially "de-Japanize" their own traditional way of managing companies, dramatically reducing their criticism of the American way but at the same time making their own management practices less human-oriented.

44

Time Gaps as a Business Tactic

Ma wo Tsukau
(Mah oh T'sue-kow)

Encounters between foreign and Japanese business people can be frustrating for many reasons, ranging from an inability to communicate clearly and completely to the problem of different values and different goals.

One factor that is often especially disturbing to inexperienced American businesspeople in particular is the Japanese concept and use of *ma* (mah), which can be translated as "empty spaces", meaning periods of time when everything stops and in the Western sense there is no progress; no forward movement.

The Japanese sense of and use of *ma* originated in Zen Buddhism. It was honed to perfection by samurai, became an integral facet of Bushido, and still today is a significant part of typical Japanese behavior.

To Japanese, *ma* is not actually a blank space in time. It is filled with meaning that is determined by the situation. Cultural authorities in Japan say its primary use is to allow the participants in a discussion or negotiation time to define and understand the real intentions of the other party through "feeling the atmosphere created by the words."

This is an awfully esoteric concept for the typical foreign businessperson to understand and accept.

In business and diplomatic encounters, *ma* is a way the Japanese have devised to cope with the demands of ambiguity. When these encounters are among Japanese, the fact that they are all on the same cultural channel gives them the ability to "read" the blank spaces and reach conclusions.

Foreigners who are not skilled in the cultural telepathy of the Japanese can be left wondering what is going on and what they can do about it. Too often, their typical reaction is to talk longer and louder, both of which the Japanese regard as impolite, if not insulting, and indicative of a low order of culture.

The area of Japanese culture where *ma* plays a major role, and is far easier for the foreigner to understand and accept, is in the appreciation of haiku poetry and the traditional arts and crafts of Japan, from architecture, literature and music to painting.

To fully understand these media, readers, listeners and viewers must take time, stop time, and let the objects and sounds speak to them in the "language of silence."

The Japanese use of silence as a means of communication goes well beyond the *ma* concept. There is, in fact, a key word, *chinmoku* (cheen-moh-kuu), that refers specifically to "silent communication."

Chinmoku means silence that is tinged by reticence and taciturnity, and is another cultural characteristic that was especially associated with the samurai. Samurai were taught that remaining silent was better than speaking because silence was more powerful than speech. It contributed to harmony and order by not contributing to disorder, and encouraged thoughtful reflection, etc.

Another aspect of *chinmoku* in the samurai code and in the common culture of the people was the hierarchical structure of the society. One had to be extremely careful not to use the wrong language to a superior, criticize a superior in any way, or appear to be disrespectful in any way, so remaining silent, particularly in any kind of formal meeting or gathering, was the safest thing to do.

Because the feelings of people could be hurt so easily, speaking in vague terms—or not speaking at all—became a cultural trait that is still manifested today in most formal situations as well as in advertisements. As a rule, the Japanese are turned off by big talkers, by people who are verbally aggressive, and by advertisements that shout at them. [The most effective advertisements in Japan are those that are designed to elicit warm feelings and spiritual satisfaction.]

The Japanese reluctance to speak up is the reason why they typically never ask questions or comment in any way at lectures, leaving Western speakers, especially Americans, mystified and frustrated by the lack of response. There is a major effort going on in Japan now to encourage the Japanese to speak up at such gatherings, international conferences, etc., but this is an uphill struggle against powerful cultural programming.

Interestingly, and fortunately, Japanese culture is much more accepting of women being big talkers, and they are famous for it. This cultural variation has been a very positive factor in the emergence of a growing number of women business leaders in Japan since the last decades of the 20th century. *

---

* On an *aisatsu* visit to see an ailing business lady who was in her 80s at the time and noted for her ability to talk, I asked her how she was doing. She glared at me and said loudly: "The only thing that still works is my mouth!" She talked almost non-stop for the next hour, causing her nurse to tell me to leave.

Experience shows that silence from a Japanese individual, company, organization or the government can have a number of meanings, from embarrassment to disinterest or the lengthy process it takes for them to reach a decision.

Understanding which of these messages is being sent requires a great deal of cultural insight, patience, and skill in discovering the real meaning of *chinmoku*.

The Japanese also commonly use silence as a means of "killing" proposals. This well-known practice, which is especially popular with politicians and diplomats, is known as *mokusatsu* (moh-kuu-sot-sue), which is translated as "killing with silence"—something that is well known in the West, where it is generally considered both unprofessional and impolite.

It behooves Westerners dealing with the Japanese to be aware of their use of *ma*, or time gaps, and turn this Buddhist-samurai trait into a positive factor by silently reviewing what has just transpired, or quietly discussing the proceedings up to that point with team members, and confirming or formulating new plans for the next time segment of the presentation or dialogue.

45

The Discriminating Mind

Urusai no Hitotachi
(Uu-rue-sigh no Ssh-toh-tah-chee)

Most of the arts and handicrafts that are associated with traditional Japan were originally imported from Korea and China—or to be more accurate, were brought to Japan by Korean (and occasionally Chinese) immigrants.

Already ancient in China and on the Korean peninsula, these arts and crafts had achieved a high level of form, finish and overall quality that is now regarded as fine art. Over the following generations, the descendants of these immigrants, using the master-apprentice approach, continued to raise the level of the aesthetic and functional elements of their crafts, resulting in taste of the Japanese becoming more and more discriminatory.

From the 14th and 15th centuries on, the samurai, steeped in Zen concepts of simplicity and elegance, took the discriminatory faculty of the Japanese to the connoisseur level.

The Japanese remain today among the most discriminating

people on the planet—not only in their view of physical things, from cell phones to "bullet trains," but also in their view of the way things should be done, what is right acceptable and what is not.

Most of the qualities that the Japanese look for in products, processes and ideas are subsumed in the word *ki* (kee), which has a variety of related meanings, including "spirit, nature, heart, care, feelings, precaution, mood, flavor and atmosphere," depending on how it is used.

When something meets the criteria of *ki* it is said to be *ki ni iru* (kee nee ee-ruu), which means it is agreeable, suitable, acceptable, pleasing. *Ki* may also be used in reference to people. A *ki ni kuwanai* (kee nee kuu-wah-nigh) person is someone who doesn't taste right.

Although the *ki* programming of Japan's younger generations is much less powerful that what it was in the past, it is still discernible even in younger Japanese because so much of it is built into the language and the culture. They simply absorb it.

Between 1960 and 1990 many of the failures of Western products in Japan were precisely because they did not meet the *ki* expectations of Japanese consumers. Virtually all of the products that did finally succeed in Japan first had to be Japanized.

It is still important, and sometimes imperative, for foreign companies wanting to sell their consumer products in Japan to first determine how the goods are perceived by the Japanese, and if indicated, make whatever changes are necessary to satisfy their unique *ki*.

The same advice pertains to the character and personality of foreigners in Japan as expatriates, as well as to their relationships with the Japanese. Those who do not conform to the dictates of *ki* are at a serious disadvantage.

This long history of intensive training in work skills, combined with the application of a high order of aesthetics in their arts and crafts, imbued the Japanese with extraordinarily high standards, adding to the role of *ki* and giving a new meaning to the old term *yakamashii* (yah-kah-mah-she-ee), which originally mean noisy or boisterous, but now has the additional meaning of being fastidious and choosy to a fault.

Urusai (uu-ruu-sigh) is another term that originally meant something or somebody who was persistently annoying, or troublesome, and over time came to mean someone who was characteristically fastidious and fault-finding. The most specific word for someone who is especially strict and exacting where appearance and quality are concerned is *kibishi* (kee-bee-she).

Generations of cultural conditioning in aesthetics and in the manufacture and use of handicrafts that had been turned into arts made the Japanese the most *urusai* people in the world. Japanese consumers and shoppers carefully considered and examined every product they wanted to buy. They automatically scanned it with a built-in "cultural probe" that penetrated to its essence. If there was any flaw or any weakness in the material, the design, or the fabrication of the product, the fault registered instantly and the Japanese consumer rejected it.

One of the aspects of the *urusai* character of Japanese consumers was that they expected the whole product to be "finished" and "detailed." That is, they expected the insides, the bottoms, and other areas of products that are generally not visible to also be "done."

Present-day Japanese remain among the most *urusai* consumers in the world, but as with so many other traits that they inherited from their samurai past, their fastidiousness is being tempered by the new times.

Still, it is common to hear the phrase, *shumi nado ni urusai* (shuu-me nah-doe nee uu-rue-sigh), meaning "fastidious in taste", "fussy", "meticulous" to describe Japanese shoppers, and they are still far more discerning and selective than run-of-the-mill con-sumers in other countries.

Here is another situation where many American managers and workers alike can improve their quality standards and their ability to compete in the world by emulating the exacting standards of Japan's samurai, its artists and craftsmen, and its consumers. Europeans, on the other hand, have had their own high quality standards for gener-ations, and have not had as far to go to succeed in Japan.

46

The Nihonteki Factor

Nihon-rashisa no Yosoh
(Nee-hone-rah-she-sah no Yoh-soh)

Despite its geographic proximity to Korea and China, and intermittent trade and cultural relations with these two countries for more than fifteen hundred years, Japan has been virtually isolated from the rest of the world throughout most of its history. During this long period, the Japanese developed a way of looking at things and doing things that distinguished them from all other people.

In the 1950s a relatively small number of American and European manufacturers of consumer and industrial goods began approaching the Japanese market. The failure rate among these foreign companies, especially the American firms, was startling. There were numerous government and other institutionalized barriers against foreign products coming into Japan, but there was one element in these failures that the foreign manufacturers did not anticipate and for the most part were unable to cope with.

This element, which was above and beyond the low quality and packaging of the products, particularly those that were made-in-America, was their "foreign essence." They were too "foreign" in design, shape, size, and "spirit" for Japanese tastes—something that most of the foreign manufacturers couldn't understand and couldn't do anything about.

For the next decade and more, foreign companies struggled to learn what "Japanese taste" was and how to please it. Those who did not take on Japanese partners often failed in this attempt as well. Much of the traditional taste of the Japanese is bound up in the word *Nihonteki* (Nee-hone-tay-kee).

I began writing extensively about *Nihonteki* or "the Japaneseness" of Japanese products in the late 1950s—what it was, how it developed, and why it was critical to selling in Japan, but my preaching had no discernible effect for the first decade.

The *Nihon* in *Nihonteki* means Japan. *Teki* means "suitable, fit, compatible, conforming to" or "similar to." While you can translate *Nihonteki* as "Japanese-like," it means more. It refers to the design, the quality and the essence of the product.

To be *Nihonteki* a product must adhere to several Japanese standards that are described by such words as *shibui* (she-booey), *wabi* (wah-bee), *sabi* (sah-bee), and *yugen* (yuu-gain)—concepts that make up the world of Japanese aesthetics and have been an integral part of Japanese culture since the great Heian era (784–1180).

Shibui means restrained, refined. *Wabi* means simple, quiet, tranquil. *Sabi*, literally rust, refers to the beauty of age. *Yugen* means mystery and subtlety. For centuries these attributes were the foundation of all Japanese arts and crafts, including architecture, garden landscaping, pottery, ceramics, flower arranging, kabuki, etc., and all were aspects of Japanese culture that were exemplified by the tastes and demands of the samurai class.

Korean author O-Young Lee, who was educated in Japan and

has written extensively about Japanese culture, says that the unique aesthetic quality in traditional Japanese arts and crafts is achieved through a process that he calls "contracting nature" by a technique known as *shakkei* (shock-kay-ee), or "borrowed scenery"—that is, using the sea, mountains, forests, clouds, rain, snow and other features of nature as design motifs.

The "borrowed nature"concept was known and used in both China and the West, but Japanese artists and craftsmen took it much further, creating an aesthetic effect that was original and distinctively Japanese. Instead of being satisfied with using *shakkei* to embellish their gardens, for example, they made "borrowed scenery" the main elements and the central theme.

Today's younger Japanese, who are no longer acculturated in the traditional concepts and are veterans of shopping trips abroad, are now more concerned about the price and basic quality of the things they buy than their cultural essence.

But despite the ongoing Westernization and modernization of Japanese society, Japan's traditional *Nihonteki* culture remains powerful enough that it will continue to play a significant role in the attitudes and buying habits of Japanese consumers for much of the 21st century.

If foreign marketers are aiming their sights at older Japanese consumers they should be aware that the *Nihonteki* factor may still be a vital element in their buying decisions, and act accordingly. In some cases today, when the produce is unique or of superior quality, creating the "right" image may be done through advertising, rather than redesigning the product.

Nihonteki is a concept that was honed to perfection by the samurai, by tea masters and by Buddhist monks who brought their Zen-enhanced faculties to bear on every aspect of life in feudal Japan. Foreign marketers who are not familiar with the word and what it means to the Japanese are at a disadvantage.

47

Building in Quality

Hinshitsu wo Takameru
(Heen-sheet-sue oh Tah-kah-may-rue)

During the fifth and sixth centuries, the Japanese were increasingly exposed to arts and crafts made by Chinese and Korean masters. They adopted and elaborated on the already ancient Chinese custom of using the master-apprentice approach to training artists and craftsmen. Boys, sometimes from the age of seven or eight, were apprenticed to skilled artists and craftsmen for ten to thirty years.

This system, continued for generation after generation, producing great numbers of master carpenters, carvers, painters, potters, and other artisans, gradually raising the level of the quality of everything produced in Japan, and imbuing ordinary Japanese with what may have been the highest quality standards in the world.

When the samurai came on the scene from the 12th century on, their highly honed tastes and demands for the best contributed further to the aesthetic level and overall quality of the country's arts and crafts. To be acceptable, a product had to appeal to the emotions, the intellect and the spirit of the viewer.

Present-day artists, craftsmen, designers, and others who are skilled in creating this special essence say the secret of their art lies in working with the nature and spirit of the medium so that the person viewing the art or craft can commune with that nature and spirit, drawing strength, feelings of harmony, and well-being from it.

When Japan was industrialized between 1870 and 1890, and the country began producing Western products, generally under the direction of foreign importers, the Japanese were unable to apply their traditional quality standards because the products were new to them, were made with unfamiliar equipment, and foreign importers wanted them made as cheaply as possible.

This phenomenon was repeated following the end of World War II, but this time there was a different ending. In the late 1940s and early 1950s, Japanese engineers, in collaboration with American occupation authorities, resolved to introduce the latest quality control methods into Japan.

In 1950 the American statistical control expert W. Edward Deming was invited to lecture in Japan. Virtually ignored by American industry [until the 1980s], Dr. Deming quickly became the "God of Quality" in Japan, and had a prestigious award named after him.

In 1954 J. M. Juran, another well-known American quality control authority, gave a series of lectures in Japan. Over the next decade the Japanese wedded the quality control methods learned from these two American experts with their traditional master-apprentice approach to training and with their obsession for neatness, precision and quality. Within a very short period of time they were able to engineer and produce a stream of high-grade products that took the world by storm.

For want of a simple way of describing both the attitude and process that led to high-quality products, the Japanese began using the term *no misu* (no me-sue), from the English "no miss," meaning "no mistakes." By *no misu* the Japanese meant that absolutely no mistakes should be made in design, engineering, or production, resulting in virtually zero defects and eliminating claims, costly repairs or replacements, downtime, and so on.

Japan's Toyota Motor Corporation was apparently the first to institute a system in which any employ on an assembly line could stop the whole line simply by pulling a cord when a defect or problem was spotted, like the Stop Cords that were on old trains.

As a result of this system, when Toyota-made vehicles come off the line they are usually free of all defects. Toyota engineers and managers who came up with this concept referred to it as the *andon* (ahn-doan) system—*andon* being the traditional Japanese lamp. Pulling the cord to stop the line was the equivalent of turning on a light so the problem could be seen and fixed.

The *andon* system had a profound influence on the automobile industry worldwide, and was one of the main reasons that Japanese-made cars captured so much of the world market. [Toyota has continued to make improvements in its "just in time" system of delivering parts and components in its factories. [The Toyota factory in Valenciennes, France is so efficient that it keeps only two and a half hours worth of inventory on hand.]

Mistakes should be corrected immediately. Trying to cover up mistakes makes them more unbecoming and painful—*samurai code of ethics.*

By the 1990s, the Japanese were referring their standards of quality as *atarimae no hinshitsu* (ah-tah-ree-my no heen-sheet-suue) or quality that is normal or natural or is taken for granted. But they did not stop there. By this time, superior quality and design were no longer sufficient to satisfy a new breed of designers and engineers. They began to design and produce products that had the level of refinement and subtlety in design that had characterized Japan's arts and crafts for well over one thousand years. They referred to this approach as "sensory engineering."

Then designers and engineers labeled this new man-made consumer ethic *hai sensu* (high sen-suu), or "high sense", which meant that it incorporated and reflected a sixth sense—that it went beyond the sensual sense to satisfy a spiritual sense as well.

Another facet of Japanese culture that played a key role in their quality standards, and was epitomized by both the training and the mindset of the samurai, is expressed in the term *mikansei* (me-kahn-say-ee), which means incomplete or unfinished, and applies to all things in nature, including human beings.

The philosophy of *mikansei* included the concept that everything made or done by man as well as every person was not only subject to being improved but demanded it, and that this improvement was unending. This philosophy was one of the factors that gave rise to the Japanese concept of *kaizen* (kigh-zen), or "continuous improvement."

Because the Japanese were programmed to view everything they saw as incomplete and therefore demanding improvement, they were compelled by their culture to strive for perfection in everything they did—quite different from the American approach to quality, which traditionally has been to make something good enough that people would accept it, and stop there.

A few American business leaders began to pick up on the *kaizen* concept in the 1970s, after Japanese-made products had already replaced a number of industries in the U.S. and threatened others.* By 2000, the quality of most American-made products had been significantly increased, but in many areas it is still below Japanese standards. The concepts of *mikansei* and *kaizen* should be made required courses in the world's educational systems, as well as in worker training programs.*

Present-day Japanese are still happiest when they improve on a process, says management guru Masaru Chio (whom I have quoted before). "They are perfectionists. The slightest flaw in anything attracts their attention and they cannot rest until it is eliminated," he adds.

As a result of this attitude there is a strong tendency for the Japanese to try to improve on any job they undertake, particularly when using technology or copying products imported from abroad. They often seem to spend as much or more time on refining processes as they do on producing results. But once refinements have been made, their performance often shoots upward.

The standards of quality in the United States and elsewhere are generally based on cost, market factors, and profit. The quality of many products on the market could be dramatically improved at no additional cost (and in some cases, at less cost) by the application of Japanese-style holistic thinking, which often is no more than designers, engineers and technicians working together.

Today, pressure from cheaply made Asian as well as American imports is bringing increasing pressure against Japan's *no misu* approach to manufacturing, and there are signs that some Japanese companies are being forced to cut corners. But the Japanese should be wary of downgrading their standards. The future will belong to those who make the best products.

American manufacturers are a long way from adopting Japan's "no miss" philosophy, and the longer they put it off the more likely they are to be passed up by other countries with more exacting stan dards.

---

* I believe I was the first to pick up on the term *kaizen*, in the 1960s, and introduce it to Western businessmen. The Japanese business consultant who introduced me to the concept, Masaaki Imai, president of the Tokyo-based Cambridge Corporation, a consulting and executive recruit group, later wrote a book entitled *KAIZEN: The Key to Japan's Competitive Success*, published in 1986. He subsequently founded the Kaizen Institute of Japan, which has offices worldwide, and in 1997 published *Gemba Kaizen: A Commonsense Low-Cost Approach to Management* (McGraw-Hill Professional Book Group).

48

Quality With Sex Appeal

Miryokuteki Hinshitsu
(Me-rio-kuu-tay-kee Heen-sheet-sue)

Superior design and functionality were not enough to satisfy the Japanese compulsion to build quality into their products. As early as the 1980s Japanese designers and engineers began to concentrate on the idea of taking the quality of Japanese products beyond the physical into the metaphysical realm. They labeled this new level of quality *miryokuteki hinshitsu* (me-rio-kuu-tay-kee heen-sheet-sue), or "quality with sex appeal."

Miryokuteki is the word used to describe women who are especially attractive in a sexual, provocative way, and its use came naturally to the Japanese designers because there had been a sensual element in Japan's crafts for more than a thousand years.

The subsequent success of many Japanese products in world markets can be attributed in part to the sex appeal that is built into them. The French and Italians have also been good at building sex appeal into their products for a long time.

But Americans were slow to catch on, despite their obsession with using sex to sell products. By the first years of the 21st century, however, American-made cars, personal accessories and a range of other items had the unmistakable *miryokuteki* appeal.

This provides hope that American industry in general will soon reach a quality level that will allow it to compete successfully with Japan and other Asian countries steeped in art and craft traditions that go back five thousand years.

49

Business Mentors

Bijinesu Mentah
(Be-jee-nay-suu Men-tah)

Japan's ancient master-apprentice approach in arts and crafts and the more recent master-novice approach to martial arts training utilized by the samurai have been carried over into corporations. It is customary for new employees to be taken under the wing of experienced managers, technicians and engineers who are responsible for making sure that they learn the physical routines of their work, as well as the corporate philosophy and morality.

This mentoring is not incidental or casual. It is taken seriously by the mentors and the newcomers, and in more strict companies covers the gamut of human relationships and behavior, including appropriate demeanor as well as appropriate attire.

Companies and organizations now not using the mentoring system certainly should adopt it as early as possible—making as sure as possible that it is devoid of company politics. The effect on morale, efficiency and productivity can be amazing.

50
Group-Consciousness

Shudan-Ishiki
(Shuu-dahn Ee-she-kee)

Few people in any country have ever been more *shudan ishiki* (shuu-dahn ee-she-kee), or "group conscious", than Japan's samurai. They were distinguished by their apparel, by the swords they wore (and could use!), by the virtually absolute authority invested in them, and by their unique attitude and behavior.

The samurai in turn imposed absolute group-consciousness on the common people, within each of the three lower classes—farmers, craftsmen, and merchants—prescribing the occupations they could follow, where and how they lived, the clothing they wore, and their public behavior; even the level of language they used when interacting with the samurai.

The legacy of this cultural conditioning remains discernible in present-day Japan, especially among bureaucrats, educators, students, doctors, lawyers, the police and other professions, as well as among sections and departments in companies and other organizations.

This group-consciousness is characterized by *aun no kokyo* (ah-uun no koh-kyuu), which can be translated as "the ability to think in unison." It is the common cultural knowledge that makes it possible for members of a group to know what to do and how to do it without being told. It includes all of the etiquette that makes up the Japanese way, from who sits where to bowing, passing out name cards, and negotiating.

Japanese do not have to consciously think about engaging their *aun no kokyu* sense. It is always turned on, and works automatically. When new recruits enter Japanese companies, most of the attitudes and behavior they are expected to exhibit are not verbalized or given to them in the form of written instructions. They are expected to pick up on these things through their *aun no kokyu*.

Foreigners who go to work for Japanese companies often feel isolated, misused, and abused because they are not familiar with the concept and practice of *aun no kokyu*, and they are not capable of "plugging into" the right cultural channel because they are not intimately familiar with Japanese culture in the first place. A great deal of the Japanese behavior that Westerners find contradictory, confusing, or simply irrational, is a result of the Japanese *aun no kokyu* sense in action.

Philosopher Tomonobu Imamichi says that in Japan you cannot be part of a group unless you have suffered the same troubles in the same way as everyone else in the group. He adds that these experiences include both the good and the bad, and that these experienced-based bonds are the source of the psychological unity of the Japanese.

The Japanese have the use of group-consciousness down to a science, and it is most often seen in the famous *go-nin gumi* (go-neen guu-me) or Five-Person Group, whose antecedents goes back to ancient times when the whole country was divided into groups of five households for control and tax purposes. Each of these groups was responsible for order within the group and for ensuring that all of the laws and customs of the land were followed.

In the Western world group-consciousness is most often demonstrated in sports teams whose members have been drilled in all of the routines they are expected to perform. Some foreign companies and other organizations use the team approach the same way the Japanese do.

It is a well-proven method of getting the most out of people—physically, intellectually and spiritually.

51

The Right Thing
the Right Way!

Subete ni Jouseki ari
(Sue-bay-tay nee Joh-say-kee ah-ree)

The first commandment in the Bushido code of ethics is generally listed as rectitude, meaning moral uprightness, correctness in intellectual judgment and behavior, and justice. What this commandment was designed to do was to ensure that the samurai always did the right thing, the right way, at the right time.

Because the samurai created and enforced the standards of behavior that controlled all Japanese for many centuries, rectitude became the ideal standard of the common people as well. Of course, this code of behavior—buttressed by Confucian, Shinto and Zen precepts—consisted of doing the right thing the right way as prescribed by the samurai culture; not behavior based on objective, universal principles.

By 1700 the samurai culture covered virtually every aspect of the lives of the common people. There were precise rules of what was to be done and how it was to be done, and this distinctive way of doing things had became as codified among ordinary people as it was among the samurai.

Still today the Japanese automatically respond to situations that are based in large part on the samurai legacy of rectitude—doing things the prescribed cultural way. When these ways are rational and positive—such as attention to detail, efforts to totally master a task, a compulsion for order, harmony and quality—the Japanese have a conspicuous advantage over people whose mindset and behavior is less structured, less disciplined.

I highly recommend the introduction of kendo, karate and Zen meditation practices from Japan into the public school systems around the world. This would result in people becoming more focused and more efficient in their attitudes and behavior, without unduly constraining their ability or will to act as individuals.

As modern-day businessman-samurai Michihiro Matsumoto says, "It's the discipline that makes the difference."

"We in the West worship freedom and individualism. This includes the freedom to be mediocre. Nothing in our society assures that we will grow up with discipline and pride. Fortunately, many of us participate in an extracurricular activity, such as sports, or drama, where we learn the value of training and discipline. And many of us are fortunate to encounter a coach, teacher, or pastor who instills a sense of responsibility to the team or the greater whole. But many of us fall through the net, and our lack of a common "Bushido" type ethic means that our lowest common denominator is quite low indeed in many areas of public behavior, responsibility, and service."—*Joe Schmelzeis.*

52

The Design Advantage

Dezain de Sa wo tsukeru
(Dezain day Sah oh t'sue-kay-rue)

The end of Japan's feudal system in 1945 released the creative talent of the people for the first time in their history. One of the elements of this talent was a samurai-honed cultural trait described by the word *arasagashi* (ah-rah-sah-gah-she), which translates nicely into English as "nit-picking."

In other words, the samurai and eventually all Japanese were culturally conditioned to look at all things, especially forms and functionality, with critical eyes, and to be compulsive about correcting any flaws or weaknesses they perceived.

The tea ceremony, with its strict form and emphasis on the beauty of the utensils used, was both an expression of these built-in traits and a way of exercising them. The purpose of the tea ceremony was to purify the mind and put the soul at rest.

This new freedom to create as they pleased, combined with the *arasagashi* trait and their long history of striving to achieve perfection in their handicrafts, gave the Japanese special cultural advantages as designers.

In addition to these built-in cultural advantages, the Japanese also have nearly two thousand worth of artistic motifs to spur their design efforts. This combination of talent and artistic heritage was one of the major contributing factors in Japan's dramatic rise to economic prominence.

The lesson to be learned from this facet of Japanese culture, past and present, is that making ongoing aesthetics and artistic training an integral part of a nation's culture has extraordinary benefits, and is something that should be made universal.

Adds old Japan-hand Glenn Davis: "Mind-over-matter techniques are excellent tools for concentration, especially when one is involved in a creative process. It is well known that samurai used *zazen* (zah-zen) meditation techniques to prepare themselves for battle. These same techniques could be used by Westerners to prepare themselves for taking tests, designing new products, building self-confidence, etc."

Recognition of the power of design is obviously a cultural thing; an aesthetic thing as well as a functional thing. While this facility has been relatively well developed elsewhere in the world for centuries, including in primitive societies, it did not really show up on the mind screen of American manufacturers until Japanese products began to make significant inroads into the American market in the 1970s.

The "coming out party" in the U.S. for the power of design was a cover story by that title in *BusinessWeek* magazine in 2004. The story elicited responses from numerous design firms in the U.S., pointing out that there was much more depth and breadth to the "design revolution" in the U.S. than *BusinessWeek* suggested.

However, it was not an epiphany of aesthetic appreciation that brought on this new-found interest in good design. It was the hard demands of business, and the fact that a growing number of product designers realized that American industry virtually ignored the experience and insights of consumers.

In Japan, well-designed products resulted from built-in aesthetic as well as functional imperatives that were universal in the culture. It seems that this connection was not made in the U.S., and then only on a miniscule, isolated scale, until the 1980s. [One of the earliest successful "power design" products: Apple Computer's *PowerBook laptop*, tracked by Design Consortium in Worthington, Ohio.]

I have maintained for a long time that culturally speaking the U.S. is just now approaching the level of sophistication that the Japanese achieved during their Heian period (794–1180).

53

The Aesthetic Factor

Biishiki
(Bee-ee-she-kee)

As the centuries passed, the samurai were more and more enjoined by their code to conduct their lives in a simple, elegant manner, and to demand simplicity and elegance in the arts and crafts—a way of life expressed in several concept words that are part of the *Nihonteki* factor mentioned earlier, as well as *wabi* (wah-be), *sabi* (sah-bee), *shibui* (she-booey), *yugen* (yuu-gain) and *myo* (me-yoh).

Wabi emphasizes the simple, the austere, the serene, the asymmetrical, and the imperfect. *Sabi* means rust and refers to an aged or antique look. *Shibui* means astringent, rough. *Yugen* expresses both a mystery and a subtlety that lies beneath the surface of things. *Myo* refers to a special spirit that imbues the truly beautiful.

All of these concepts had their origins in Buddhism, especially Zen Buddhism, which became the instruction manual for the samurai lifestyle and code of ethics.

From the 16th century on, with no wars to fight, Shoguns and provincial lords took the lead in promoting aesthetic practices. Shoguns began imitating the cultural practices of the Imperial Court in Kyoto. Fief lords began imitating both the Imperial Court and the Shogunate Court in Yedo. Samurai retainers, as well as a growing class of affluent merchants, followed their examples. Over the generations, the aesthetic practices that had originated in the Imperial and Shogunate Palaces spread among the common people.

Not allowed to work in ordinary jobs, the samurai spent their time honing their martial skills in hundreds of *dojo* (doh-joh), or martial arts halls, that sprang up throughout the country; and engaging in the arts and in literature, especially poetry, calligraphy, and the tea ceremony. Thus the appearance of many samurai who were as noted for their scholarship and poetry as for their fighting skills.

In fact, Japan appears to have been the only country in which *bigaku* (bee-gah-kuu), aestheticism, became an integral part of the culture, taught and practiced as an essential part of the national character. While the tea ceremony was the most focused of these customs, others that were universally practiced included flower-viewing, moon-viewing, and beautiful-sight-viewing.*

The Japanese emphasis on aesthetics naturally carried over to their arts, crafts, architecture, interior decorations and apparel. Still today, aesthetic appreciation is a significant part of the lives of most Japanese, and continues to impact on everything they do.

This is another area in which Americans in particular are weak. We have no recognized standards for beauty in man-made things.

---

* By the 8th century many places in Japan had become famous for their natural beauty, celebrated in poetry and other literature. Viewing platforms were built in many of these areas to provide nearby residents and visitors with a place to sit, eat and drink while enjoying the scenery.

The importance of aestheticism in life is not officially or formally recognized, and is not practiced by a significant percentage of the population.

This is another aspect of the samurai code of ethics that should be emulated by the rest of the world.

54

Using the
"Water Business"

Mizu Shobai wo Tsukau
(Me-zoo Show-by oh T'sue-kow)

There are, I believe, more drinking places in Japan than in any other country, and they play a direct and significant role in business, in politics and in Japanese life in general.

Traditionally this voluminous "night-life" was euphemistically referred to as the *mizu shobai* (me-zoo show-bye) or "water business"—harking back to the Shogunate days when bathhouses were centers for drinking and indulging in other forms of recreation and entertainment. But these hot pillow bathhouses were only a small percentage of the drinking establishments that appeared soon after the founding of the Tokugawa Shogunate in 1603.

In addition to restaurants that served *sake*, there was a nation-wide network of redlight districts and so-called geisha houses, and thousands of inns in the country, all of which served as drinking establishments.*

By 1700, the samurai [who were not allowed to work at regular jobs] were sharing the pleasures of the country's *mizu shobai* with well-to-do merchants and their profligate sons. And without office buildings or common meeting places, the samurai and the merchants used the drinking establishments as their meeting venues. [The plotting that brought down the great Tokugawa Shogunate in the 1860s was done in the *mizu shobai*.]

From the last decades of the 1600s on, large numbers of urban Japanese have repaired to drinking establishments at night to unwind, get to know each other, say what is really on their minds and enjoy each other's fellowship. Not only political matters, but business and personal matters as well have traditionally been resolved in drinking and eating establishments.

The *mizu shobai*, with the addition of thousands of coffee shops in the late 1940s and 1950s, continued to serve as the primary meeting place for Japan's businessmen and politicians until the appearance of additional office space [that was air-conditioned] and more private telephone lines from 1960 on. But that was not the end of the "water business."

The extraordinary growth of business in Japan from 1952 to 1970 resulted in a comparable growth of the *mizu shobai*. Businessmen and politicians spent several billion dollars a year in the *mizu shobai*, stroking each other, building and nurturing rela-

---

* Japan was the first country in the world to have a national network of roadside inns. By 1650 there were clusters of inns at post stations along all of the five main roads leading to Yedo (Tokyo), spaced one day's march apart, to accommodate the great number of people who traveled there by foot for the remaining 218 years of the Tokugawa era. Hundreds of other inns were located around hot spring spas, on scenic coastlines and rivers and alongside and over fast-flowing streams in mountain gorges. On the *Tokkaido*, or Eastern Sea Road, the main road between Yedo and Kyoto, there were 111 luxury inns for fief lords and other elite personages, sixty-eight annex luxury inns for important people of lesser rank, and 2,905 inns for the samurai troops that accompanied the fief lords, and for ordinary travelers.

tionships, and, in fact, making their overly structured, overly formal, excessively *kata*-ized system work by bringing in the human element.

The ongoing importance of the *mizu shobai* is based to a considerable extent on the fact that it is only when drinking in informal settings that the Japanese can dispense with the rigid etiquette that controls their speech and behavior, and, poetically speaking, let their hair down.

Fortunately, Japan's *mizu shobai* etiquette is similar enough to the etiquette of the Western world that inexperienced foreigners are able to enjoy it and achieve some of its positive benefits. It is often *only* in the "water business" that Japanese and Westerners find that they have enough common ground to persevere in attempting to establish worthwhile business relationships.

This comes with a caveat, however. There is generally a great deal of pressure for people to drink heavily, especially at parties and other celebrations, and especially when newly met foreigners are concerned. The reason for this latter fact is that the Japanese have traditionally believed that you cannot really get to know people until they get drunk because it is only then that their true personality and character emerges.

It is difficult for visitors to spend very much time in Japan without getting in involved in numerous drinking sessions, and refusing to drink while everyone else is determined to get tipsy, dispense with etiquette and have fun, can be awkward for both sides, and may be construed as impolite or devious by the Japanese side if there is no acceptable excuse.

One reason for abstaining that is usually acceptable is that you are under doctor's orders not to drink. If you do drink but want to control the amount, it is a good idea to simulate drunkenness (to whatever degree that is appropriate for the occasion) after only two or three drinks. It is not a good idea to try to compete with Japanese hosts drink-for-drink.

While the size and importance of the *mizu shobai* has shrunk since the 1990s, it remains a major industry and continues to play a significant role in creating and maintaining business relationships.

Westerners who ignore or are not aware of the importance of the "water business" in Japanese culture are at a disadvantage. Those who inform themselves and become skilled at using the *mizu shobai* find that it can be a major asset and can often mean the difference between success and failure in doing business in Japan.

55

Present-Day Female "Samurai"

Gendai no Onna Samurai
(Gane-die not Own-nah Sah-muu-rye)

Positive elements in the samurai code of ethics were not the only cultural assets that helped Japan recover from the destruction of World War II and become an economic superpower in less than three decades. Japanese women played an equally vital role.

By the mid–1960s (after having taking up residence in Japan in the late 1940s) it became obvious to me that Japanese women were more resilient, more practical and more flexible than Japanese men (a characteristic they share with other women around the world), and that most of the more desirable lifestyle changes that had occurred in Japan since the end of the Pacific War in 1945 were initiated by women, or were made successful by women.

In fact, being more susceptible to cultural pressure than men, Japanese women in general had been influenced more deeply by the

Bushido code of Shogunate Japan than male commoners, and were more representative of the positive elements of the samurai code of ethics than the men.

In other words, Japanese women were more selfless, more caring, more honest, more diligent, more faithful, more trustful and more courageous than the men. Japanese women were in fact so different from Japanese men that they often seemed to be the product of different cultures.

There are still two worlds in Japan: the male world and the female world. Although in many respects women continue to live in their own dimension, there are now doors between the two dimensions and more and more women are crossing over to the business side of the men's world.

Foreign companies in Japan were the first to take advantage of the special skills, flexibility and ambitions of Japanese women. Among other things, Japanese women have proven to be far more adept at learning foreign languages than men, making them especially valuable in the international business arena.

In addition to the entry of millions of Japanese women into industry in the usual "female" type occupations, there are growing ranks of samurai-like women whose courage, talents and diligence have taken them to high positions in business, politics and the professions.

Having the advantage of both their *bushi* (buu-she) heritage and their female mentality, Japanese women will no doubt play an increasingly important role in the future of Japan, and in doing so, serve as role models for women in other countries who have not yet emancipated themselves from the gonad-driven dogma of men.

Samurai females were trained to be as resolute as the males, including sacrificing their lives and the lives of their children at a moment's notice. During the warring years [much of the 15th and 16th centuries], samurai were required by their lords to bring back the heads of enemies they had killed in battle. It was one of the duties of female members of samurai families to wash and apply cosmetics to these severed heads in preparation for presenting them to their lords.

56

Singing as a
Business Skill

Utau ga Bijinesu Sukiru
(Uu-tah-uu gah Bee-jee-nay-sue Suu-kee-rue)

One the most popular type of bars in Japan today—and one of its most successful cultural exports—is the *karaoke* (kah-rah-oh-kay) bar, or bars that provide microphones, sound equipment and tape-decks for patrons who want to sing to the company of orchestra-like music.

Karaoke means "empty orchestra," and refers to the illusion that the singer is performing with a live orchestra. There are thousands of such bars in Japan, and it is a matter of personal pride that everyone who goes into such a place tries his or her hand at singing. Many Japanese practice singing several songs in private (often for years) so they won't be embarrassed when they are called on to perform in karaoke bars or other public places.

Performing in a karaoke bar means more to most Japanese businessmen than just having a good time. Besides relieving stress and providing personal satisfaction, such performances are seen by many as important to one's overall character and personality—as an accomplishment that is similar to such traditional but now rare arts of calligraphy, and composing haiku poetry, which traditionally were marks of cultural attainment.

In explaining the importance of the karaoke bars to foreign guests, Japanese businessmen will often say that you must understand karaoke in order to understand the Japanese, and that if you truly want to communicate with them you must learn how to sing along with them as well as perform on your own. There is a great deal of validity to this firmly held and often expressed belief, which obviously accounts for the number and popularity of such bars.

The fact that very few Westerners, particularly present-day Americans, can carry a tune, much less sing decently, is a social and business handicap when they are in Japan (and in Korea*). My advice is to learn at least one song, even if it is as simple as "Old Grey Mare" or "I've Been Working on the Railroad."

NOTE: karaoke is pronounced kah-rah-oh-kay, not kerry-okie!

* Singing is even more deeply imbedded in Korean culture than in Japanese culture. Ancient Chinese officials sent on missions to the Korean peninsula recorded that it was the custom of Koreans to gather around out-door fires in the evenings and sing for several hours. One of the reasons for this custom was that singing was part of an institutionalized emotional and spiritual cleansing process called *suyong*. Koreans have their own equivalents of karaoke bars as well as *kisaeng* houses where singing is part of the entertainment. Korea's *kisaeng* houses are the equivalent of Japan's geisha houses, but are some one thousand years older.

57

Japan's Saints

Nihon no Seijin-tachi
(Nee-hone no Say-ee-jeen-tah-chee)

In early Japan every generation had men whose character can only be described as saintly. They represented all that was best in the teachings of Buddhism, Confucianism and Shinto. Most of these men were not born into wealth and power, and those who were, often gave them up. As a result of their character, these *seija* (say-ee-jah), or saintly men, were sought out by the high and low alike for their advise on matters of all kinds.

The conditions that produced this long line of saintly men changed dramatically after the fall of the samurai system of government in 1868, but here and there the values that made such men persisted—not only among the ex-samurai but also among the new class of educator-scholars, industrialists and statesmen.

Remarkably, the early decades of the 20th century, when Japan was roiled by fanatic militarism, also gave birth to a few saintly men, particularly in the business world. Some of the names that immediately come to mind are Konosuke Matsushita, Sazo Idemitsu, and Makoto Shinto. When Shinto visited the American White House in the 1980s, President Ronald Reagan later said he was the most saintly man he had ever met.

Still today Japan's cultural heritage, especially as exemplified by the most humane and enlightened samurai, tends to make successful men more philosophical as they age, with some becoming more saintly in their attitudes and behavior.

The more successful and older Japanese men become, whether businessmen, professionals, or yakuza gang leaders, the more they are inclined to assume a soft, gentle, innocent stance that perhaps can best be described as Buddha-like. How much of this Buddha-like character is make-believe and how much is real is often beside the point. Their image of virtuous selflessness gives them an aura of charm and charisma that vastly increases their power because people look upon them as saint-like, incapable of evil, and therefore people who can be trusted to say and do what is best for everyone.

[Western businessmen, diplomats, and politicians encountering such formidable figures should keep in mind that even Buddhas have agendas, and an unwavering will to win in the end.]

Saintly individuals, both men and women, also appear in American and European cultures, but they are rare in the business and political worlds. Sainthood, it seems, is incompatible with Western style capitalism and politics. This suggests that it might be unwise for Japan to continue down the road to pure capitalism, and that some fundamental changes in Western cultures could make them a great deal more humane.

58

The Advantage of Having Eight Million Gods

Happyaku Man no Kamigami wo Mikata ni suru
(Hop-p'yah-kuu Mahn no Kah-me-gah-me oh
Me-kah-tah nee sue-rue)

There are said to be eight million "gods" in Shinto, Japan's indigenous religion, and I count this as one of the luckiest breaks that could have befallen the Japanese.

With power and authority spreading among that many divinities—none of whom were all seeing, all knowing, and all powerful—it is no wonder that the Japanese have never been religious in the Western sense and never lost sight of the physical aspect of reality.

Buddhism arrived in Japan in the 6th century and gradually spread among the people. But, with one major exception, it did not preach or practice violence in a physical or metaphysical sense.*[1] Militant Christianity was introduced into Japan in the 1540s and it had some initial success [primarily because some of the southwestern fief lords wanted the guns and trade that came with it], but it achieved power only over a small percentage of the people and was virtually eradicated some one hundred years later in a bloody massacre at Shimabara castle, near Nagasaki.

A new flood of Christian missionaries flocked into Japan in the second half of the 19th century, certain that they would be able to convert Japan's millions to Christianity. They also had some success in spreading some of the humane social tenets of Christianity but not its theology, which is infantile compared to Shinto and Buddhism, or its dogma about women and human sexuality, which are irrational and inhumane.

As a result of their resistance to Christianity, the Japanese as a national group have never suffered the anguish of Original Sin, never been scourged by murderous priests, never been attacked for their religious beliefs, and never been psychologically and physically tortured by the repression of their sexual impulses.*2

One of the special cultural, economic and political advantages that Japan has today is that it is not driven by religious conflicts. This, added to the enduring legacy of its samurai heritage, gives Japan an opportunity to have a positive influence on the world that goes well beyond its economic prowess.

---

*1 Some time after Buddhism was introduced to the Imperial Court, the emperor ordered all of the provincial lords to build temples in their domains for its propagation. The Court later began awarding excess members of the royal family with major temples, along with peasants and tax-free lands to support them. Some of these temples grew into huge complexes, and began to arm and train their hundreds of monks to fight to protect the temples and the treasures they had accumulated. By the 16th century, some of the temples in the vicinity of Kyoto, the imperial capital, had become so big they could field armies of monks, and began raiding the city. Oda Nobunaga, the paramount warlord of the time, finally attacked and defeated the militant monks, ending their power.

*2 Since the three largest "Western" religions—Christianity, Islam and Judaism—are cults by definition, the world would be much better off if all non-Asian countries adopted Buddhism and Shinto. [The main difference between Christianity, Islam and Judaism and the small cults with their bad reputations is that these three cults are very big and very powerful, and therefore have been much more successful as imperialistic dictatorships.]

References to Shinto having eight million gods and to the ribald nature of some of its enduring festivals are likely to give an entirely false impression of the depth and scope of Shinto. I want to dispel that image immediately. Shinto is, I believe, the most profound and wisest of all so-called religions. It is based in part on the scientific foundation of the origin, nature and activity of matter and anti-matter that is just now beginning to be understood by the most advanced professionals in the fields of physics and quantum physics—facts that are unknown to most Japanese themselves.

If anyone doubts this claim, I recommend that they read *The Looking Glass God: Shinto, Yin-Yang, and a Cosmology for Today*, written by then young philosopher Nahum Stiskin, and published as an Autumn Press Book by Weatherhill in 1971–2. Stiskin writes that the ancient Chinese principle of yin and yang is one of asymmetrical polarity, and that asymmetrical polarity and dualistic monism are the foundations of Shinto.

Shinto relates to the creation of the cosmos out of the void, how matter consists of patterns of vibrating energy, how matter behaves on an atomic and sub-atomic level, how life evolved, and how all life forms are made of the primordial energy of the creation, that all matter, from stars and planets to human beings, are in a constant state of recycling.

For some of his insight into Shinto, Stiskin went to the *Kojiki* (Koh-jee-kee), or "Record of Ancient Matters," Japan's oldest extant chronicle, recording events from the mythical age of the gods of creation to the time of Empress Suiko (593–628). The *Kojiki* consists of three sections. The first one covers the creation of the cosmos (along with the earth and Japan!). The other two sections cover historical events of the Suiko era.

The reason why Shinto has not been recognized for what it really represents is that its tenets are expressed in terms of the gods of this and the gods of that, and in other symbol references, because the scientific terms to express its foundation in physics didn't exist at that time. The extraordinary scientific knowledge in Shinto was apparently arrived at through tapping into the cosmic knowledge bank.

Among other profound things, *Kojiki* refers to the spiral helix, which is present in DNA, in other body cells, in hair, and on up the chain to the Earth and the Cosmos at large. Shinto also includes a precise formula for human beings to maintain harmony between their physical and spiritual halves, which involves keeping the energy in the body flowing properly.

This formula consists of cold-water bathing, a proper diet (take that, Atkins fans!), the use of salt, and meditation.

Says Stiskin: "Shinto has never had a social or ethical dogma with which it indoctrinates its adherents. It relies solely upon the intuition and judgment of the individual and views society as the product of the combined expression of so many individuals.

"Emphasis is laid upon the individual's achievement of harmony with the flow of natural law with his personal life, within his family, and consequently within the entire national and world community. Once inner mental and physical harmony is achieved within the individual, harmony on the wider social scale must naturally emerge."

59

Summing Up

Matome
(Mah-toh-may)

Still today doing business in Japan is essentially an exercise in Japanese culture. The more you know about the culture and the more skilled you are at using it—from the language and the etiquette to its philosophical, aesthetic arts, craft, festival and recreational traditions—the better able you are to conduct business successfully.

Generally, the most successful Japanese managers are those who are so steeped in Japanese culture that they are inspiring figures. They epitomize the samurai-like character and personality that the Japanese have been taught to admire, respect, and follow willingly.

These individuals often command fierce loyalty because of their cultural virtues, not because of any intellectual brilliance, technical knowledge, or skills they may have. Many of them are not exceptionally intelligent, but they often have remarkable common sense, strong wills and the courage to pursue goals regardless of the difficulties involved.

Rather than book learning or years of practical experience to provide them with insights and guidelines, these Japanese managers intuitively tap into a bank of cultural knowledge that transcends technology and scientific processes, and puts everything into human terms.

As noted earlier, the Japanese are not the only ones who are impressed by such cultural masters. Foreign government leaders and businessmen by the score have been so taken by the charisma, the magnetism, of these outstanding men that they were virtually mesmerized.

Despite fundamental cultural charges that have occurred in Japan since the 1950s, there is still an abundance of Japanese businessmen who have the equivalent of master's degrees in cultural administration (MCA's) rather than MBA's. They continue to play significant roles in both the domestic and international fields of business.

It is important that Westerners doing business in and with Japan be aware of these MCA's, have some appreciation of where they are coming from, and learn how to deal with them from a cultural and human as well as a business perspective.

In fact, one of the first lessons the outsider must learn about doing business in Japan is that it is a very personal, very emotional thing—far more so than doing business in the West. It therefore requires a great deal more human investment than what is common in most Western countries.

I do not recommend that foreigners attempt to "go native" in doing business with the Japanese. The main reason for not going native is that if one speaks the language fluently and behaves exactly as the Japanese do, there is a strong tendency for them to treat you the same way they treat other Japanese, and that is a major disadvantage. There are far too many negative factors in the traditional Japanese way of doing things for the foreigner to deliberately burden himself or herself with this aspect of the culture.

Fortunately, the Japanese are also culturally programmed to automatically treat non-Japanese, particularly Westerners, as guests, generally with all of the more positive implications that are inherent in the term—something that most non-Asians in Japan for any length of time learn quickly and thereafter use to their advantage.

In fact, this guest syndrome kicks in automatically at the sight of a non-Asian face, even though the individual concerned may have been born in Japan and never lived anywhere else. Despite the many aspects of Japan's culture that foreigners find admirable and satisfying, being treated exactly like a Japanese is not one of them.

It is not recommended, however, that foreigners take unfair or malicious advantage of the guest syndrome of the Japanese. Polite, thoughtful, generous, and rational behavior should be the rule at all times. The Japanese are very much aware of most of the negative facets of their culture. Most are making a genuine effort to eliminate them and be more rational and positive in their conduct. And obviously, the positive traits that the Japanese inherited from their samurai ancestors far outweigh the negative factors.

However, as Donald Westmore, Executive Director of the American Chamber of Commerce in Japan, notes, for Japan to become fully integrated into the world economy, as they so often claim is their goal, the Japanese must overcome the irrational aspects of their mythical self-image and their belief that they cannot change their way of thinking and doing things.

Westmore recalled that as late as the 1960s there were claims by the agriculture industry that the Japanese couldn't eat rice not grown in Japan because their stomachs were different, and that the sporting goods industry claimed that the snow in Japan was different from snow elsewhere, so imported skis wouldn't work in Japan.

"This narrow Japanese view of themselves has widened considerable since those days, but the belief that they are unique in the world is still just below the surface, and regularly manifests itself in ways that are detrimental to their future and their relationships with the rest of the world," Westmore said.

"The positive facets of the samurai legacy do, in fact, give the Japanese an extraordinary advantage, and it is that aspect of their traditional culture that should be emphasized—not the myopic views of the past," he added.

Sums up Japan-based journalist, author and educator Glenn Davis: "One of the most important messages that Bushido could have for modern Americans in particular would be the way it teaches politeness and respect for elders and superiors. This is something that Americans with the "I don't give a damn" attitude should learn. Just realizing that a layer of politeness and respect acts as a social cushion, preventing much of the friction of daily life, would be a step up from the in-your-face confrontational style that is so prevalent in modern America.

"All samurai were taught never to use Bushido in an offensive manner, only for self-defense. This way of thinking goes far beyond martial arts and is a philosophy in itself."

While this is certainly true, the samurai were also taught that when they did engage in battle the goal was to win. Japan's present-day samurai businessmen are steeped in the philosophy of winning, and in the Bushido skills that contribute to success.